Holy Trinity
Evangelical Lutheran
Church Library

Y0-CLD-442

A CHILD'S STORYBOOK
OF BIBLE PEOPLE

A CHILD'S

SHERI DUNHAM HAAN
Martha Bentley, Illustrator

STORYBOOK
OF BIBLE PEOPLE

BAKER BOOK HOUSE, GRAND RAPIDS, MICHIGAN

Copyright 1973 by Baker Book House Company
ISBN: 0-8010-4077-9
Library of Congress Catalog Card Number: 73-76202
Printed in the United States of America

First printing, June 1973
Second printing, December 1973

TO
CHAD AND SHELLY
TWO PRECIOUS LITTLE PEOPLE
ON LOAN TO US
FROM
GOD

PREFACE

A Child's Storybook of Bible People was written to acquaint children with men, women, and children in the Bible, for the biographical accounts in the Bible play an important part in understanding God's plan of salvation. The unusual and very interesting ways in which God dealt with His people hold a special fascination for young children.

Several features were incorporated into *A Child's Storybook of Bible People* at the request of those who used *Good News for Children* and were kind enough to provide me with their comments, suggestions and questions.

Although Bible chronology is not easily grasped by young children, the stories in each of the three sections of this book are in chronological order. Short, simple plays and a few children's songs are included, both of which can be used in family devotions or classroom instruction.

Another new feature is the inclusion of rhythm stories, which may be read as poems. However, a new dimension will be added if a leader chants one line and a group chants the line back, all the time clapping a rhythm. Further explanation of this technique appears on page 10.

The large print and expressive drawings were used to attract the young reader. The simple, biographical style appeals to the very young listener.

Young children can and should be included in family devotions. The book was first of all written for family devotional use but teachers can effectively use the stories, songs, plays, and rhythm stories as enrichment materials.

I pray that God may use *A Child's Storybook of Bible People* to speak to His little ones so that they learn to praise Him always, everywhere, and for everything. We'll praise Him together!

Sheri Dunham Haan

CONTENTS

CHILDREN OF THE BIBLE   **12**

Jesus Loves Children   15
Song: Jesus, Friend of Little Children   17
The Dreamer   18
A Big Sister Helps   21
Moses   28
A Voice in the Night   30
The Boy Who Killed a Lion and a Bear   34
Song: Only a Boy Named David   37
David and the Giant   40
Little Helper   41
Josiah, the Child King   47
The Christmas Baby   50
Song: Away in a Manger   52
The Little Teacher in the Temple   54
One Lunch Feeds Thousands   57
The Death of a Daughter   60
Sound Asleep in Church   64
Boy Detective   68
Song: Jesus Loves Me   72

WOMEN OF THE BIBLE   **74**

The First Lady   76
She Looked Back   78
The Red Cord   80
The Lady General   85
A Prayer for a Baby   92
A Planned Escape   98
A Feast in the Wilderness   101
Bread for Tomorrow   106
Jars and Pots All Over   110
A Surprise Gift Twice   113

CONTENTS

An Angel Visit	122
Praising God at Eighty-four	124
Praise God, I Am Healed!	128
Who Gave More?	130
A Gift at the Well	131
Song: Jesus Gave Her Water	136
A Foot Bath	138
Mary!	140
Song: We Welcome Glad Easter	142

MEN OF THE BIBLE — 144

The Time the World Drowned	146
Kiss and Make Up	148
Rags to Riches	153
The City that Crashed	164
The Mightiest Man	166
Whirlwind to Heaven	175
Rescue by Rope	179
A Strange Place to Spend the Night	185
John the Baptizer	188
The Graveyard Monster	192
The Bold Fisherman	197
Song: I Will Make You Fishers of Men	202
The Plan that Healed a Friend	214
Song: Ten Lepers	216
Just One Came Back	218
Song: Zaccheus	220
A One O'clock Miracle	223
Death of a Friend	227
Just in Time	229
Empty Chains	231
Earthquake at Midnight	235

RHYTHM STORIES

Children have always loved rhyme and rhythm. They enjoy hearing the lilt of rhyming words and recalling them in rhythmic beats. For this reason several rhythm stories have been included in this book.

Rhythm stories may be read simply as rhyming poems. However, they have a cadence that naturally calls for clapping. Only a small group is necessary to do these rhythm stories, but they may also be used successfully with a group of twenty or thirty children. One member should be the leader who sets the clapping rhythm. A quick tempo is best and it should be maintained throughout the story. The leader first claps his hands on his knees and then claps his hands together. The group repeats the rhythm with the leader and then the leader chants the first line of the story to this rhythm. The group chants the same line back to him. Then the leader chants the second line and the group chants it back to him. The rhythm story continues in this manner.

To help you get the feel of the rhythm, the syllables in the rhythm stories have been divided into beats and placed in columns. Most of the stories will have eight beats to a line; however, sometimes more than one syllable is said to a beat.

A sampler record is included with this book so that you may hear Mrs. Haan and a group of children doing some rhythm stories.

Rhythm stories are for group involvement, for enjoying God's Word together. There are no more powerful stories than the ones God included in His book, the Bible. Read them. "Rhythm" them. Rhyme them. Love them!

	Page
Moses	28
David and the Giant	40
The Christmas Baby	50
The Little Teacher in the Temple	54
The First Lady	76
She Looked Back	78
Who Gave More?	130
A Foot Bath	138
The Time the World Drowned	146
The City that Crashed	164
A Strange Place to Spend the Night	185
A Plan that Healed a Friend	214
Just One Came Back	218
Death of a Friend	227

Jesus Loves Children	15
Song: Jesus, Friend of Little Children	17
The Dreamer	18
A Big Sister Helps	21
Moses	28
A Voice in the Night	30
The Boy Who Killed a Lion and a Bear	34
Song: Only a Boy Named David	37
David and the Giant	40
Little Helper	41
Josiah, the Child King	47
The Christmas Baby	50
Song: Away in a Manger	52
The Little Teacher in the Temple	54
One Lunch Feeds Thousands	57
The Death of a Daughter	60
Sound Asleep in Church	64
Boy Detective	68
Song: Jesus Loves Me	72

OF THE BIBLE

JESUS LOVES CHILDREN

Mark 10:13-16

The disciples were tired. It had been a very warm day. And Jesus had been sitting on the hillside for a long time. While He was busy talking to the people, fathers and mothers kept coming up to Him. One lady walked right up to Him with her brand new baby girl who was kicking and crying. Another man led his son who was just learning to walk. Two more little ones came crawling. Their chubby hands reached for His toes. A great big boy came running right through the crowd.

The disciples were so upset. They began whispering. "Why are these children being brought to Jesus now? Can't these parents see that Jesus is very busy?"

"I guess they want Jesus to touch their children."

"I know. But He's so busy right now. We'd better stop them before anyone else comes to bother Him."

Then they turned to the parents. "Now, sit down, all of you. Can't you even wait until Jesus is finished?"

Jesus stopped talking right in the middle of His sentence. He frowned when He looked at the disciples. He spoke harshly to them. He sounded almost angry. "Don't ever keep the children away from me. Let them come. My kingdom is filled with them. In fact, anyone who wants to be part of my kingdom must love me and trust me to take care of him the way that little children trust their parents to care for them."

Jesus, busy Jesus, wanted the children near Him. He loved them. He spoke softly to them while He held them closely in His arms. Jesus felt their little fingers reaching up to touch His face. He saw their bright, sparkling eyes. Jesus blessed them. Jesus loved the children so very much, just as He loves you!

THE DREAMER

Genesis 37:1-11

Joseph was one of the babies of a big family. His father thought Joseph was quite a special child. Sometimes father Jacob did extra things for his little boy. He bought Joseph a beautiful coat. It was very colorful. There were many pieces of cloth in it. It was also quite expensive! You can almost imagine how bright it was . . . made of orange, purple, red, yellow, green, and magenta. It was so much nicer than any coat the other boys had. This made them very jealous of Joseph.

One night Joseph had a dream. He dreamed he and his brothers were in the field. Each one of them was cutting grain. When each brother had cut a large pile, he tied the grain together. Joseph's bundle of grain stood up, proud and straight and tall. But the other brothers' bundles bent way down in front of Joseph's. It was like they were bowing to it.

But there was one thing the brothers didn't know. God was working in Joseph's life. When he was much older, he would become a powerful and important man. And each one of the brothers would be under Joseph's rule. So Joseph's dreams were not just funny or pretend; they were sent by God!

A BIG SISTER HELPS

Exodus 2:1-10

MOTHER: Miriam, pick up Moses. Hurry! Better rock him a little while. We've got to keep him quiet.

MIRIAM: Okay, mom. How long before you'll have that basket done? He cries so loud! Sh! Little baby. Sh-h-h!

MOTHER: Well, Miriam. It's dry now. And it doesn't leak. I just tried it out in a big pot of water. All I have to do is put some soft blankets in it.

MIRIAM: When will we bring him to the river?

MOTHER: In an hour or so, whenever he's settled down and sleeping. We'll also have to wait and see how many guards are around.

MIRIAM: (whispering) Sh-h, little Moses. Please don't cry. Boy, mom, I guess we will have to be careful all right. We sure don't want Moses thrown in the river. He's too sweet.

MOTHER: I'm finished with the basket now. We'll wait and see what father says. Rock Moses to sleep if you can, Miriam. I'll start breakfast. Oh, . . . Miriam, . . . remember, dear, to pray that God will watch over our little Moses. God is the only one

	who can keep our little boy safe.
MIRIAM:	All right, mom. (singing) Hush, little baby, don't you cry . . .
NARRATOR:	Mother and Miriam talk it over with father. After breakfast they decide that it's time to bring Moses to the river. Carefully they put him in the basket. Miriam puts the covers around him. Mother double checks everything. Father watches outside the house. Then Mother picks up the basket. Miriam skips along ahead of her, watching and looking for guards. When they get to the river, Mother puts the basket along the edge, in the weeds. It is early morning. The sun is just beginning to warm the shallow water.
MOTHER:	Now you stay here and pretend you're playing. But really keep your

eyes on that basket. Remember our plan?

MIRIAM: Sure do, mom. I'm ready.

MOTHER: Thank you, Miriam. You come home when you're finished.

MIRIAM: I will. Bye, mom.

NARRATOR: Miriam wades in the water along the side of the river. She hums and plays in the sand. Then she sees some people coming. It is the princess coming for her daily bath in the river. Her servant girls wade in the water with her. They come close, so close to the basket. Miriam holds her breath, waiting.

PRINCESS: Look! Right over there in the weeds. It's a basket. Hurry and get it. Hmmm, I wonder what's inside.

(The servant brings the little basket to her.) Oh, look! It's a baby. Poor thing. Hear him cry? He's probably hungry. Isn't he precious? Some mother probably put him here so he wouldn't have to drown. If I only had someone who could take care of him. He's such a little guy.

MIRIAM: I think I know someone who could help you. Should I go get her?

PRINCESS: Please do. I will need some help. He's too little for me to take care of. Hurry now.

MIRIAM: I'll be back in a jiffy. It'll take only a minute. (Miriam hurries home and gets her mom. On the way back, she tells her mom what happened.)

MOTHER: Oh, Miriam! This is God's answer to our prayers that He would help us.

MIRIAM: Isn't it great! Moses won't have to die. The princess fell in love with him right away.

MOTHER: We're almost there. I can see the princess. We must not act too excited or she'll catch on.

MIRIAM: Princess, this is the lady I told you about. She said she would help you.

PRINCESS: Thank you so much, little girl. I'm glad you brought this lady. (She turns to look at Mother.) Are you willing to take care of this little child? I will pay you for your work.

MOTHER: Yes, I'd be very happy to care for him.

PRINCESS: Well, that's good. You just take him home with you. He can stay at your house until he's old enough

27

to come to the palace. Now be sure that you take good care of him. He's my new little son!

NARRATOR: Mother picks up Moses and the three of them go home. They can't wait to tell father everything that happened. And they surely remembered to thank God for giving them a plan to keep Moses from being killed.

A RHYTHM STORY — rhythm stories are explained on page 10.

MOSES

Exodus 2:1-10; 3:1-10

King	Phar-	oah	made	an	or-	der
To	kill	the	lit-	tle	boys.	
Mo-	ses'	mom	had	quite	a	job
To	hush	his	ba-	by	noise.	

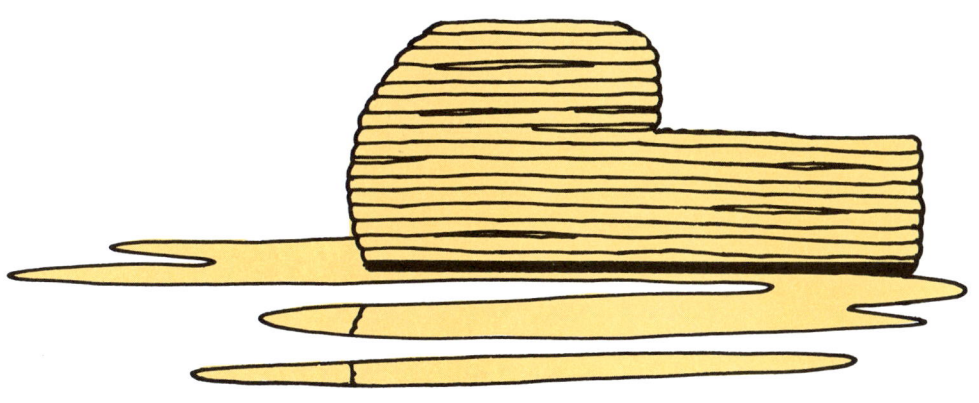

Soon Moses' mom got busy
She made a special boat;
She put her baby in it,
Then put it out to float.

Pharoah's daughter found him
And took him as her son.
So Moses was a prince
And was taught to live like one.

When Moses became older,
God called to him one day;
"My people now are slaves,
You will help them get away."

God had this job for Moses
Ever since he was a boy;
God had told His people
He would turn their tears to joy!

29

A VOICE IN THE NIGHT

I Samuel 3

Hannah was thrilled! God had sent her exactly what she'd asked for . . . what she'd been praying for. In her arms she held a baby boy! Because God gave him to her, she named him Samuel.

While Samuel was still a very small child, his mother brought him to God's house. This wasn't just for a visit. He was going to live there. Elkanah, Samuel's father, and Hannah were keeping a promise Hannah made to give their baby boy to God. So they brought him to the temple. He lived with Eli, the priest.

Hannah didn't forget her little boy. Not for a minute! Every year she made him a new coat. When she came to the temple, she brought it to him. She loved to hear Samuel talk about his jobs at the temple. He was such a big help to Eli.

One night, Samuel was sleeping but he jerked

awake when he heard a voice, "Samuel, Samuel."

Immediately he jumped up. He knew that Eli was old and could not see very well. In fact, he was going blind. So Samuel hurried to Eli's room. "I'm here, Eli. You called me."

"No, Samuel. I didn't call you. Now go back to bed."

Just when Samuel was settled in bed again, he heard, "Samuel, Samuel."

Quickly he ran to Eli again. "Here I am. I heard you call me."

"No, no, my son. I didn't call you. Now go back and lie down."

Then it happened the third time. "Samuel, Samuel."

So again he hurried to Eli. "You called me? I'm here!"

Eli hadn't called. But he was quite sure he knew who had been calling. "No, Samuel. I didn't call you. Go back to your bed. If you hear the voice again, it will be the Lord. Tell Him to speak and that you will listen."

Samuel hurried back. He snuggled under the covers. Then he heard, "Samuel, Samuel." It was just like before.

Samuel sat up in bed.

"Speak to me, Lord.

I'm listening."

Then the Lord told Samuel a lot of things. He told him what was going to happen in the future. He told him what would happen to Eli. Then Samuel knew that God wanted him to be a prophet, to warn people. This was the first time God had talked to Samuel. And Samuel was sure that it wouldn't be the last!

THE BOY WHO KILLED A LION AND A BEAR

I Samuel 17:34-37

*King Saul would not let David fight the giant. David was just a boy.
And Saul thought he was too young.
He thought that David didn't know how to fight. So David told Saul what had happened when he was a little boy.*

King Saul, when I was really a young boy I used to take care of my father's sheep. Now that may not seem like a big job to you, but sometimes it was very hard.

I will never forget this one day. The sheep were looking for grass. I was playing music for them on the little flute I used to carry. All of a sudden I heard one little lamb crying. I jumped up so fast that I dropped my flute. I looked around quickly. I saw a lion with a lamb in its mouth. The lion was a big one . . . at least it looked awfully big to me!

I ran just as fast as I could. My heart was pounding hard. When I came close to the lion I slowed down. I crept up closer and closer. Then I pulled the lamb from the lion's mouth. All the time I was praying to God. I knew I needed His help.

Just as I pulled the lamb to safety, the lion turned and pounced on me. His mouth was open wide. I had to try to kill him bare-handed. I grabbed for him. My hands caught his tangled beard. As I was fighting, I was praying. God helped me. I felt so strong. My muscles felt big and tough. As I caught the lion's wooly beard, I flipped him over on his back. Quickly I killed him with my bare hands.

Then came a bear. He must have been hungry too because he tried the same thing. Just as quickly as before I grabbed the lamb from his teeth. Then I pulled open those huge, wide jaws. I tugged and pulled. At last I killed him too.

35

God was with me. If he could help a little boy kill a lion and a bear without an arrow or a spear, he will certainly help me fight this giant!

ONLY A BOY NAMED DAVID

Arranged by R. J. Hughes

On-ly a boy named Da-vid, On-ly a lit-tle sling, On-ly a boy named Da-vid, But he could pray and sing; On-ly a boy named

ACTIONS: 1—extend right hand, measuring height. 2—rotate right forearm clockwise. 3—fold hands in prayer. 4—imitate flowing water. 5—raise right hand with fingers outstretched. 6—hold up one finger. 7—clap hands sharply. 8—point to forehead. 9—drop or slump down.

©1957 by Zondervan Music Publishers. All rights reserved. Used by permission.

38

in the sling, And the sling went round and round; And round and round and round and round and round and round and round, And hit the giant in the head And the giant came tumbling down.

A RHYTHM STORY — rhythm stories are explained on page 10.

DAVID AND THE GIANT

I Samuel 17:34-37

Young	Da-	vid	left	his	fa-	ther's	house
With	cheese	and	grain	and	bread.		
He	was	off	to	see	his	broth-	ers
Just	as	his	fa-	ther	said.		
As	Da-	vid	neared	the	camp-	ground	
He	found	that the	men	were	scared.		
Not	one	would	fight	the	gi-	ant	
Not	one	of the	sol-	diers	dared.		
This	gi-	ant	was	Go-	li-	ath.	
He	stood	over	nine	feet	tall.		
He	shouted	and	bellowed	so	of-	ten,	
The	sol-	diers	ran	when he	called.		
Ev-	ery	day	this	gi-	ant	roared,	
"Choose a	man	to	fight	me a-	lone."		
Da-	vid	heard	all the	noise	he	made	
And	picked	up	five	smooth	stones.		

40

Young David took his slingshot
And loaded it with care.
Just as his slingstone a-round,
The first stone whizzed thro' the air.

Right between his startled eyes
That stone hit Go-liath's head.
He fell with a crash and clatter;
David killed him; he was dead!

LITTLE HELPER

II Kings 5:1-15

My name is Naaman, the commander-in-chief of the king's great army. My uniform hangs heavy with medals. They glitter in the sun. Some folks say I'm a hero. Maybe I am. But I am also a man with a problem . . . a big one. My skin is white and rotting. I have leprosy.

My wife's little servant is a girl who believes in God. She was excited and her eyes flashed when she came to my wife one day. "I wish the Commander would go see the prophet who lives in Samaria. I'm just positive he could heal this awful leprosy."

She's such a little gal, long black curls and dark eyes. She is really just a child. Yet she seemed so sure that this prophet could heal. So I decided it was worth a try.

Now I didn't know the prophet at all. So I talked to my king. He wrote a letter to the king of Israel.

> *To the King of Israel:*
> *The man bringing this letter is my*
> *servant, Naaman. I want you to heal him*
> *of his leprosy.*
> *The King of Syria*

I packed my things and took some nice gifts along. I had twenty thousand dollars in silver and sixty thousand dollars in gold. For an extra little gift, I packed ten brand new suits. I would pay almost anything to get clean, pink skin again. So with my servants, horses, and chariots I started out.

When we came to Israel, we went straight to the king. He read this letter carefully. Then he began ripping his clothes . . . yes, his red velvet robe! He moaned over and over again. "Oh, no! Why did your king send you to me? Am I God? Does he think that I can give life to people or take it away? This must be a trick. You're really going to bring your armies to our land. I'm sure you want war with us and that's the real reason for your visit. Oh! Such trouble!"

I tried to tell him that I didn't want war. All I wanted was clean skin again. Then the king received a message from a man named Elisha. He was the prophet the little girl talked about. So I took the gold and the silver and the clothes and went to see Elisha.

When I came to Elisha's house, he didn't even

come to talk to me. He sent a messenger out. This man told me to go and wash seven times in the Jordan River and then my skin would be perfectly healed.

That's when I became angry, really angry. Didn't Elisha know that I am a hero? Why should I wash in the dirty, smelly Jordan River? We've got cleaner rivers right by my own house. So I refused!

My men were waiting for me in the chariots. They could tell by the way I walked and stomped that I was furious. But they finally convinced me that I should try. I'd come this far. I guess it would be a little silly to leave now. Besides, it wouldn't hurt me to wash in that river.

I went to the Jordan River. It was a gray-brown muddy color. I stepped in. It was mucky. I could feel the slime at the bottom. I dipped in once, twice, three times, then four, five, six, and finally seven times. I came up slowly. Would it work? Could this prophet of God heal me?

When I came to the top, I opened my eyes. The water still dripped from my hair and eyelashes. I blinked to clear my eyes. I pulled out my arm. It was rosy . . . it was pink. Yes, indeed! It was as clear and beautiful as a child's skin. I ran out, checking my body. I was healed. Every single inch of skin was absolutely like new!

I hurried back to Elisha's house. I ran to him. "Elisha, Elisha! I know that God is God . . . the only God in the whole world. Please take these gifts."

Elisha didn't want the gifts. So I thanked him over and over again. When I went home I had healthy skin and a love for God in my heart. How thankful I am for our little servant girl who knew about God and believed in Him!

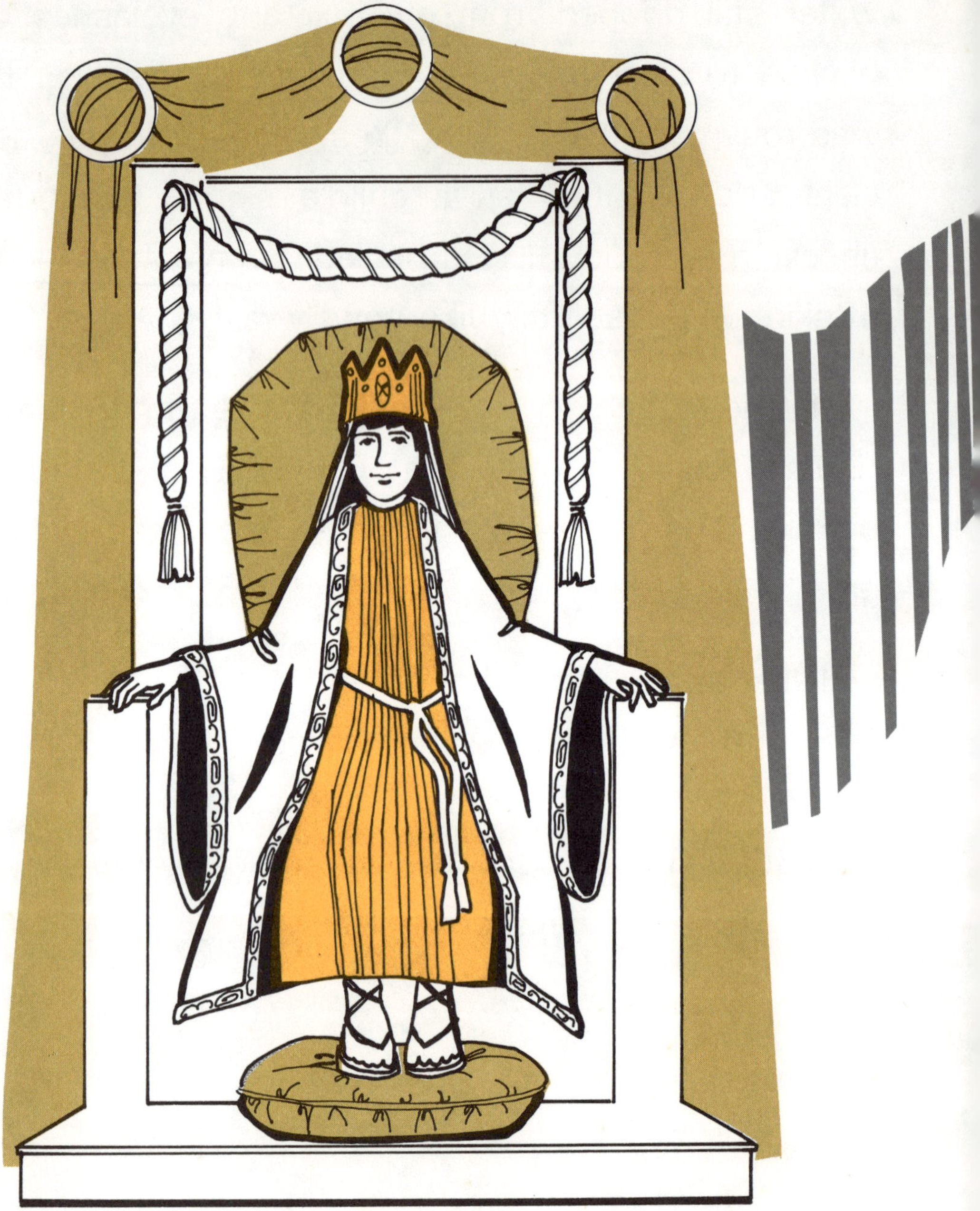

JOSIAH, THE CHILD KING

II Kings 22, 23

Josiah looked in the mirror. He saw the jeweled crown on his head. The purple velvet robe hung behind his little body. It was even hard for him to believe . . . he was king! He was the ruler of the land, and he was only eight. It took a long time for him to learn about being king. But one thing was sure. King Josiah wanted to obey God.

When Josiah was king for twelve years, he remembered the temple. The steps had crumbled.

Pieces of wood had rotted. Little boards hung out. Stones were loose. What a mess God's house had become.

Without question, the temple needed to be fixed. All the people gave money so that it could be made beautiful again. Soon there was enough money to get started and Josiah quickly gave orders. "Call for the carpenters. Bring in a bricklayer. We'll need some builders too. Order some lumber. And don't forget to bring huge piles of stone. There's a lot of work to do around here."

It's true that he was young, but he was the king. So people obeyed immediately. Many people got busy fixing the temple. Some men fitted stones all day, others sawed the lumber and fixed the rotted boards. It was a noisy place and everyone was working hard. At last the house of God was beautiful again.

While the men were working on the temple, the high priest found part of the Bible. He sent it to

King Josiah. When the king heard the words, he believed them. He called all the important men of his kingdom together. Everyone who lived in Jerusalem came too. Josiah read the Bible to them. In front of all these people he made a promise to God . . . to live as God told him to in His Word. And all the people made the same promise to God.

King Josiah also went to work on another problem, idols! He found all the statues the people were worshiping. They were their gods. And Josiah knew that there is only one true God. So he broke and burned all these idols. He wanted to be sure the land was rid of them, every single one!

Such a young king he was! But he was really wiser than most of the older kings. He was wiser because he loved and served God.

A RHYTHM STORY — rhythm stories are explained on page 10.

THE CHRISTMAS BABY

Luke 2:1-8

Jo-	seph	led	the	don-	key	out	
While	Ma-	ry	got	things	packed.		
They	start-	ed	out	for	Beth-	le-	hem
With	Mary	on the	don-	key's	back.		
At	last	they	came	to	Beth-	le-	hem
To	find	a	place	to	stay;		
But	ev-	ery	room	was	packed	so	full,
They	slept	in a	barn	on the	hay.		

50

Later on that quiet night,
Mary had a baby boy.
It happened just as God had said;
Mary's heart was filled with joy!

Isn't it strange that God's own Son
Would come in such a special way?
God sent His Son to earth for me
I celebrate it Christmas Day.

AWAY IN A MANGER

CRADLE SONG

William J. Kirkpatrick, 1838-1921
Harmonized by R. Vaughan Williams, 1931

1 A-way in a man-ger, no crib for a bed,
2 The cat-tle are low-ing, the Ba-by a-wakes,
3 Be near me, Lord Je-sus; I ask Thee to stay

The lit-tle Lord Je-sus laid down His sweet head.
But lit-tle Lord Je-sus, no cry-ing He makes.
Close by me for-ev-er, and love me, I pray.

The stars in the bright sky looked down where He lay,
The little Lord Jesus asleep on the hay.

I love Thee, Lord Jesus! Look down from the sky
And stay by my cradle till morning is nigh.

Bless all the dear children in Thy tender care;
Prepare us for Heaven, to live with Thee there.

Harmonization from *Enlarged Songs of Praise*. Used by permission of Oxford University Press.

53

A RHYTHM STORY — rhythm stories are explained on page 10.

THE LITTLE TEACHER IN THE TEMPLE

Luke 2:41-50

The	donkeys	lined	up,
The	people	had	packed;
The	children	were	ready
To	start	moving	back.
The	man	gave the	call,
"We're	ready	to	go-o!"
The	line	started	moving
Though it	moved	quite	slow.
They'd	gone a	long	way,
The	kids were	having	fun;
When	Mary	broke the	news,
"We've	lost our	son!"

They hurried back to town,
Looked up the streets and down.
They asked all a- round
But Jesus couldn't be found!

They went to the temple
After looking three days.
They found Jesus preaching.
My, were they a- mazed!

Mary scolded Jesus
For being gone so long.
But Jesus answered strangely,
"I've got to work for God."

(softly)
But Jesus answered strangely,
"I've got to work for God."

55

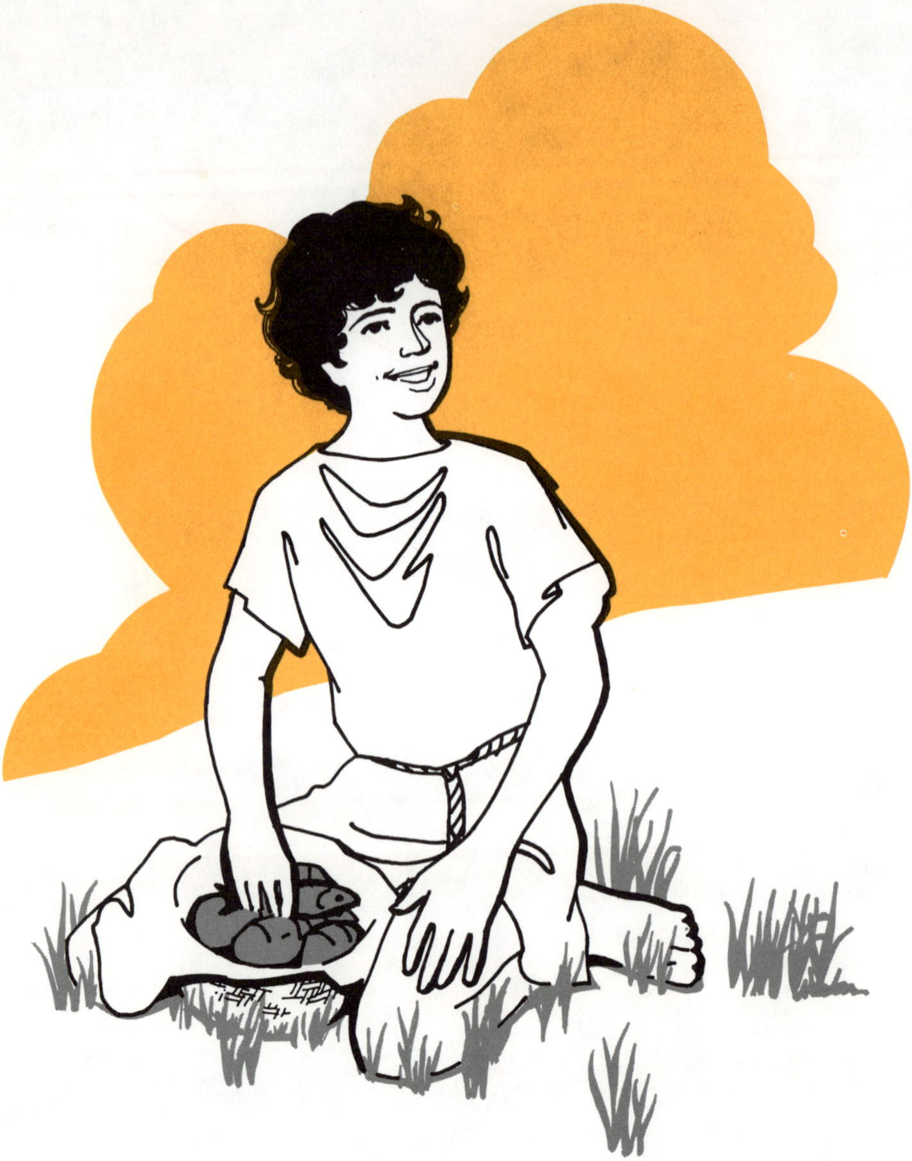

ONE LUNCH FEEDS THOUSANDS

John 6:1-14

It was a beautiful afternoon. The sun was warm. There was a cool breeze from the lake. It was a perfect day for a long walk. Mom gave me a special lunch all for myself. I saw her put in five loaves of barley bread. They were still warm and fresh. Then she put in a real treat . . . two smoked fish. WOW! This day was going to be great! I just knew it.

I picked up my lunch sack and said good-bye to the other kids. Off I went, all by myself for a change. The first thing I looked for was a straight stick to carry. I found a perfect one. As I walked I picked up two stones. They were different and pretty. Later I stopped to rest. I took out a smoked fish. I sniffed it. Boy did it smell delicious! But I decided to save it. I had only two. Besides, maybe I would be really hungry later.

As I came over the hill, I heard voices. Then I

saw the reason. There were people sitting all over the place. Not hundreds, but thousands! At first I couldn't figure it out. But then I saw a man. He was healing a little boy. Next, he made a blind man see. Then I knew for sure that this man was Jesus. I tiptoed up real close so I could see everything that happened.

The time went so fast. Soon it was getting late, way past suppertime. And I was hungry. I started to take out my lunch. Just then I heard Jesus ask Philip, "How can we buy enough bread to feed these people?"

Philip was so surprised. I could tell by the look on his face. "Feed them?" he asked. "That would take more money than all of us disciples have."

Andrew had been watching me. He said, "I see a boy here with five loaves and two fish. But that won't help much with a mob like this!"

Jesus stood up and talked to His helpers. "Tell

everyone to sit down in groups of about fifty. Get the boy's lunch and bring it to me."

When I heard that, I put my lunch back in the sack. Sure enough, one of them came and asked me for it. I was starving by now. But Jesus probably had a better idea. So I gave it to Him.

Can you imagine what happened next? Jesus took out my five little loaves and two fish. He said a prayer of thanks to God. Then He started breaking one loaf into pieces. I never saw so many pieces come from just one little loaf of bread. But they did. I saw it with my own eyes. The disciples passed out baskets full. And Jesus made all of that food from my lunch!

But that wasn't even the biggest surprise. When everyone was full, the disciples picked up the extras. There were twelve full baskets left over! Then I was positive. Jesus could heal people. He could feed them from my little lunch. He is God for sure!

THE DEATH OF A DAUGHTER

Mark 5:22-24, 35-43

Jairus looked at his daughter. Her eyes were only half open. She breathed slowly. Her cheeks were pale. How sick she was! He knew that she needed help and she needed it soon! Quickly Jairus ran off to find Jesus.

At last he found the Lord . . . in the middle of a crowd. He pushed and shoved as he hurried to get closer. When he finally got next to Jesus he fell right down on his knees. "Jesus, Jesus. Please come! Come right now. My little girl is nearly dead. If you would just touch her, she would live! Please, hurry!"

Jesus went with Jairus. It was impossible to go fast. People pushed toward Him. They reached out to touch Him. They wanted to talk to Him, to be healed. Jesus did take the time to talk with one woman. He healed her.

While Jesus was still talking with her, a servant came. "Jairus, don't bother Jesus anymore. It's no use. Your daughter is dead."

"Dead? Oh, no!" Jairus was heartsick.

But Jesus spoke tenderly to him. "Don't be afraid or worried, Jairus. Just believe."

Then He turned to the disciples. "Peter, . . . James, . . . John. I want the three of you to come with me."

When they came to the house of Jairus there was another large crowd. Only this time the people were crying and sobbing. Some were nearly screaming.

Jesus asked, "Why are you making all this noise? Must you cry so loudly? The girl isn't dead! She's sleeping."

They laughed at Jesus. Just like that the crowd changed from crying to laughing. They'd seen her.

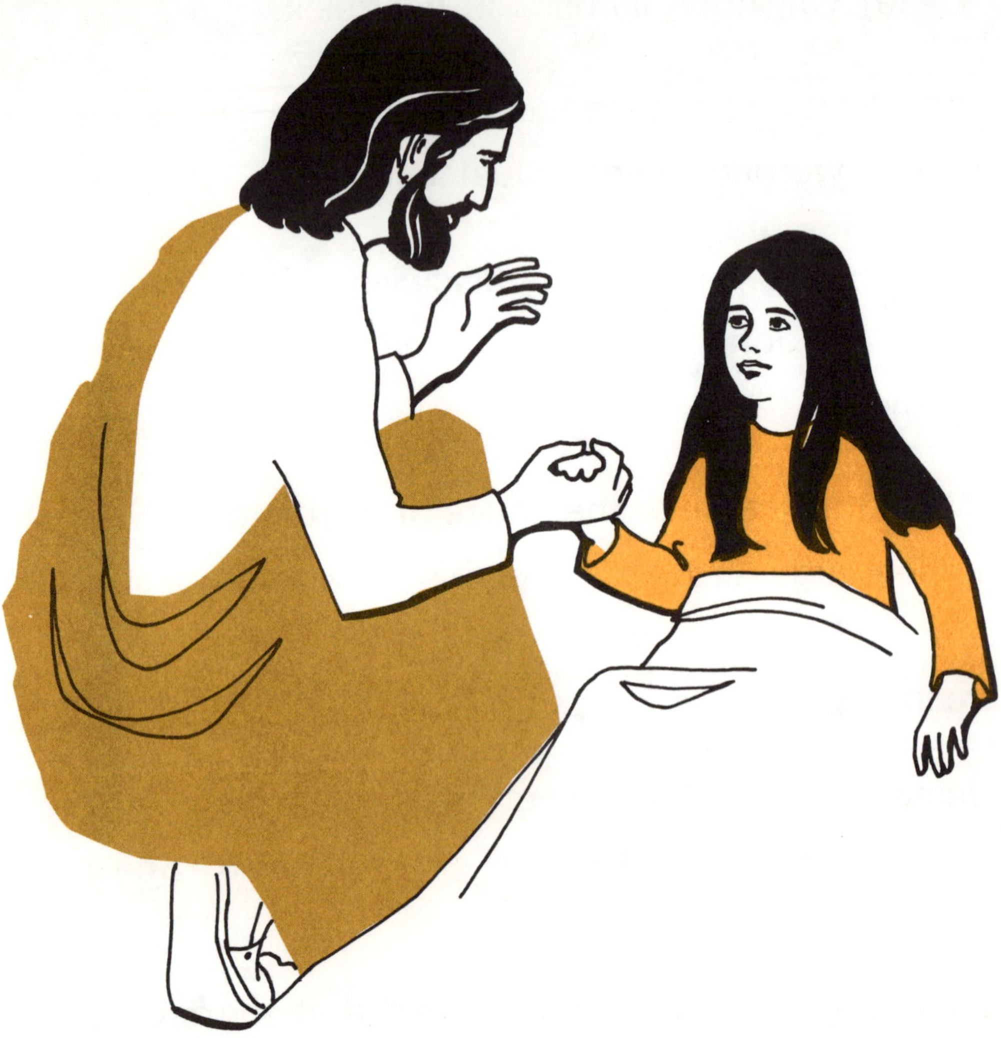

They knew she was dead. After all, she wasn't breathing!

Jesus took Peter, James, John, Jairus, and his wife and went inside the house. There lay the twelve-year-old girl. Long curls laid around her neck. Her eyes were closed. All breathing had stopped.

Walking close to her, Jesus took her hand.

"Young lady, get up."

Open came her eyes. Blink! Breathing started! She glanced around the room. She sat up. Then she got up . . . and walked! She even had supper. So quickly, in only a minute, Jesus brought her from death to life.

And her mother and father? Peter, James, and John? The crowd? Were they still laughing at Jesus? NO! Everyone was amazed. Jesus was truly master over death!

SOUND ASLEEP IN CHURCH

Acts 20:7-12

It was late, really late! Paul had been preaching for hours. The torches had been burning so long that they started to smoke. The room smelled oily. The air was fuzzy and stuffy. People shuffled so they would not get sleepy. It was past ten o'clock . . . eleven o'clock . . . twelve o'clock.

Young Eutychus was sitting on the ledge by the window. He'd been trying so hard to stay awake. He rubbed his eyes. He wiggled around. His right leg felt prickly. He got a big breath of fresh air from

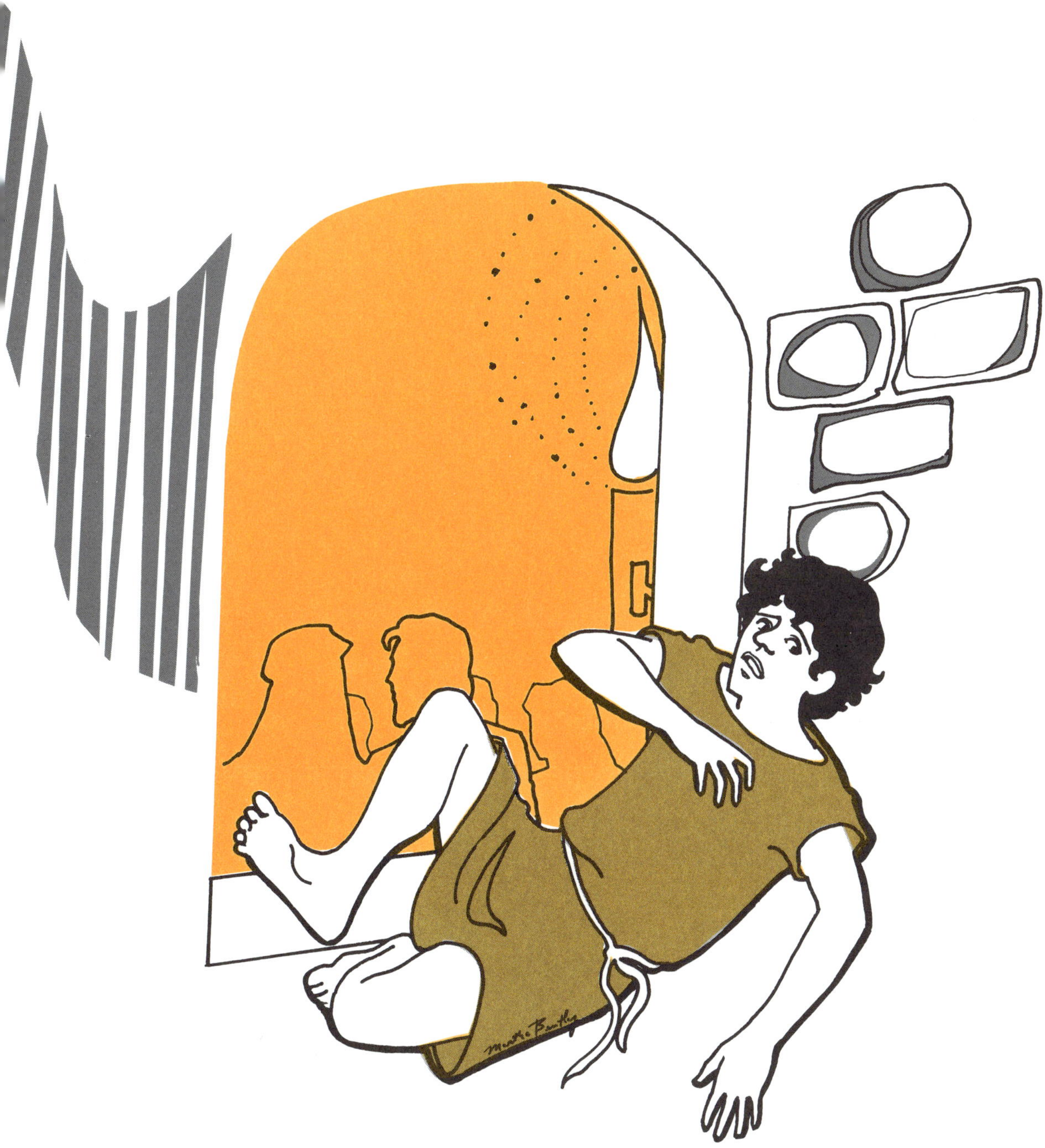

the open window. But he knew that he couldn't stay awake any longer. At last he settled back against the window. His head slowly fell forward. Finally Eutychus was fast asleep!

Hardly anyone had noticed sleeping Eutychus. He was just a lad. Certainly Paul hadn't noticed. Paul had served little pieces of bread for the people to eat. This was called "breaking of bread" or communion. And then Paul kept right on preaching. Soon it was well past midnight.

Suddenly there was a loud thump. It sounded like something fell on the street below. The lady next to the window gasped. Hurrying to put her head out the window, she whispered, "Oh, no!" On the ground three floors down lay the body of young Eutychus. He didn't move. He didn't cry or holler. He looked dead!

The people hurried downstairs. When they saw his crumpled body they were sure he was dead. Not a muscle moved, not even once. Paul pushed his way through the quiet, sad crowd. He bent over Eutychus. Then he threw his arms around the body and said joyfully, "Stop all this worrying and crying. He's still alive!"

Alive? But Eutychus didn't seem to breathe. His face was white. The people weren't sure. Carefully they brought him upstairs. After awhile they saw his fingers twitch. They waited. Then he took a quick breath. Still the people waited and hoped. A touch of pink came to his cheeks. His left knee moved just a bit. Then his lips opened. His eyes blinked twice.

The people listened to Paul and talked with him. By early morning Paul had something to eat and was ready to leave. And Eutychus? He was completely well. He talked and laughed. He felt good enough to go home! The people were relieved. It had been a strange, long night in church!

BOY DETECTIVE

Acts 23:10-24

It had been a scary night. Uncle Paul had been put in prison. There was talk around town that he would be killed. All night long I couldn't forget about my uncle. I couldn't sleep. I couldn't read or play games. This morning I couldn't eat breakfast. So I started out early to see one of my buddies.

As I walked by, I saw that the lights were on in the town hall. I heard cheers, then hushed and whisper voices coming from the building. I stopped long enough to peek in the window. There were at least forty men in there. I was ready to go on, but I was sure I heard someone say something about killing Paul. I put my ear closer to the window. I tried to keep my head out of sight. I listened closely. I shivered. It wasn't cold. I shivered because I heard something terrible!

"Mr. Chief Priest, we are going to kill Paul. We

have a plan. But we need your help. You pretend that you want to ask Paul some more questions. When the guards bring him to you, we'll be waiting along the road. Just as soon as we see him, we'll jump out of hiding. This way we can get him for sure. At last we'll be rid of him. He's such a troublemaker!" Their voices sounded so tricky and mean.

"Oh, one more thing. We have made a promise to each other. Not one of us will eat or drink a thing until Paul is dead."

When I heard that, I left. I crept away from the building. When I was farther away, I ran . . . straight to the jail. I didn't know if they'd let a young boy in to talk to Paul. But they did. I must have looked as if I had an important message for Paul. I was nervous. I could hardly get my breath because I'd been running so fast.

"Uncle, P-Paul, Listen quickly. There's a terrible plan. I just heard it at the town hall. Some men are going to kill you. They'll get you on the way to the chief priest. Probably tomorrow."

Uncle Paul didn't seem as upset about it as I was. He called the guard and asked him to bring me to the chief captain because I had something to tell him. Then Uncle Paul thanked me and we said good-bye.

We walked down the dark halls of the jail. I was glad the guard was with me. I was still a little scared. Soon we came to a big door. The guard knocked and we went in. The chief captain came and took me by the hand. Then I felt a little better. He listened carefully to what I said. Then he made me promise not to tell anyone that I had told him about the plan.

The guard brought me to the door of the jail. As he opened it, the bright light of the morning made me squint. The jail had been so dark and spooky. I nodded a thank you, then hurried home. I was safe! Uncle Paul would be safe! Now I felt like eating breakfast! Jesus had used me to help Uncle Paul.

The next day I found out that the chief captain *had* sent Uncle Paul to another, safer place at nine o'clock that very night! The captain had been very careful about Uncle Paul's safety. He sent two hundred soldiers, seventy horsemen, and two hundred spearmen with Uncle Paul just to be sure he'd arrive alive! How thankful I was that Uncle Paul was safe at last!

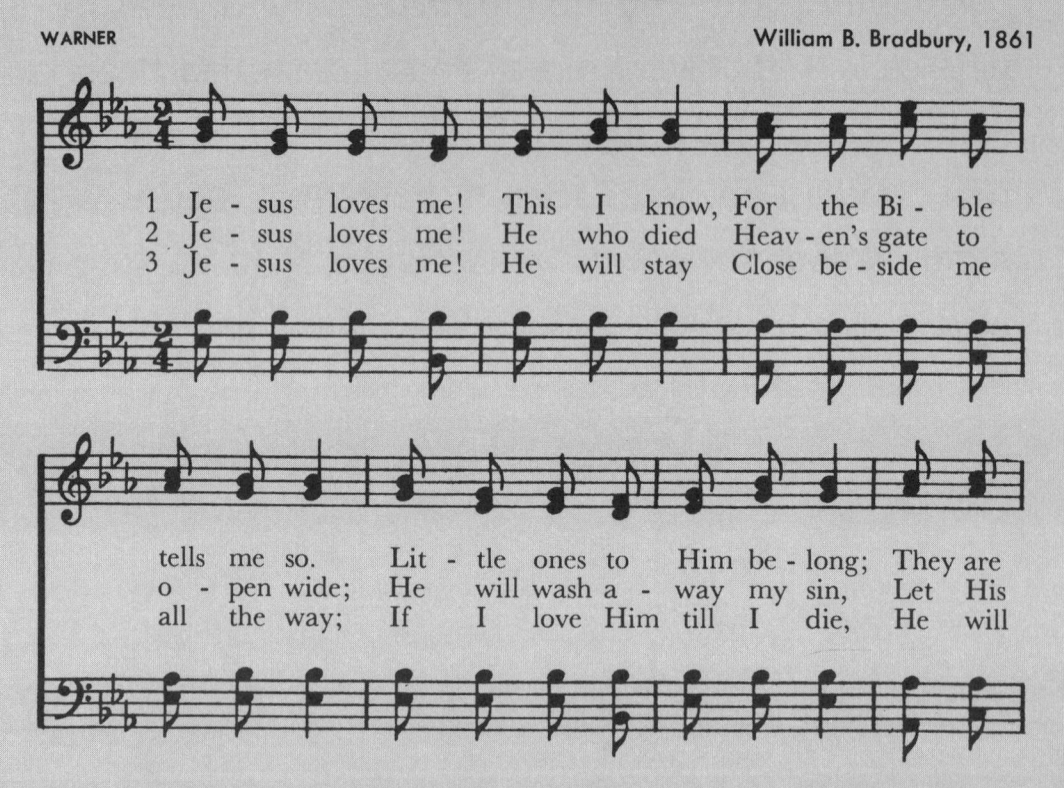

JESUS LOVES ME

WARNER

William B. Bradbury, 1861

1 Je - sus loves me! This I know, For the Bi - ble
2 Je - sus loves me! He who died Heav - en's gate to
3 Je - sus loves me! He will stay Close be - side me

tells me so. Lit - tle ones to Him be - long; They are
o - pen wide; He will wash a - way my sin, Let His
all the way; If I love Him till I die, He will

REFRAIN

weak, but He is strong.
lit - tle child come in. Yes, Je - sus loves me! Yes, Je - sus
take me home on high.

loves me! Yes, Je - sus loves me! The Bi - ble tells me so.

Anna B. Warner, 1859

WOMEN

The First Lady	76
She Looked Back	78
The Red Cord	80
The Lady General	85
A Prayer for a Baby	92
A Planned Escape	98
A Feast in the Wilderness	101
Bread for Tomorrow	106
Jars and Pots All Over	110
A Surprise Gift Twice	113
An Angel Visit	122
Praising God at Eighty-four	124
Praise God, I Am Healed!	128
Who Gave More?	130
A Gift at the Well	131
Song: Jesus Gave Her Water	136
A Foot Bath	138
Mary!	140
Song: We Welcome Glad Easter	142

OF THE BIBLE

A RHYTHM STORY — rhythm stories are explained on page 10.

THE FIRST LADY

Genesis 2:18, 21-25

When	God	made	this	great	big	world,	
He	al-	so	made	one	man;		
To	name	the	crea-	tures	He	had	made
And	care	for	His	great	land!		
Soon	God	thought,	this	is-	n't	good,	
For	man	to	live	a-	lone;		
I'll	make	this	man	fall	fast	a-	sleep,
Then	take	a	cer-	tain		bone.	

God	took	a	rib	from	Ad-	am's	chest
And	closed	the	skin	a-	gain.	first —	
Then	God	made	an-	oth-	er	man.	
A	la-	dy	for	the	man.		
God	want-	ed	her	to	help	the	man,
To	share	his	hap-	py	home;		
To	give	them	man-	y	chil-	dren,	
So	they	would-	n't	live	a-	lone.	
This	first	man's	name	was	Ad-	am,	
The	first	la-	dy's	name	was	Eve.	
When	God	looked	at	what	he'd	made,	
He	knew	that	He	was	pleased!		

77

A RHYTHM STORY — rhythm stories are explained on page 10.

SHE LOOKED BACK

Genesis 19:12-17, 26

While	Lot	sat	at	the	gate	one	night,
Two	men	from	heav-	en	came.		
They	told	him	that	his	cit-	y	
Would	soon	go	up	in	flame.		
"The	peo-	ple	are	so	wick-	ed,	
This	is	such	a	sin-	ful	town.	
The	Lord	can't	stand	it	an-	y-	more,
He's	go-	ing	to	burn	it	down."

78

Early that next morning
The angels made Lot hurry.
"Now take your wife and daughters,
You have no time to worry,"

The angels led the four away
To the gates outside the town.
Then turned and told them one more thing,
"You must not turn around!"

But while Lot's wife was running away
She looked back to see her home.
She was changed at once to pure white salt,
As dry and hard as stone.

(softly)
Just as dry and hard as stone.

THE RED CORD

Joshua 2

Rahab was just a bit nervous. She tried not to be, but it showed. She knew there were spies hiding on her roof; so she was a little jumpy. She twisted her yellow hanky in her hand. Every once in a while she jerked her head because she thought she heard someone. Or she got up to look when someone went by. How she hoped no one saw the spies come into her house. If she ever got caught hiding them, she'd be killed for sure. It scared her just to think about it.

Suddenly she heard men's steps. It sounded like heavy boots, maybe army boots. The footsteps came right to her door. When she heard a knock, her whole body jerked. From outside she heard loud voices calling. "King's guards here. Open up!"

Rahab took a deep breath. She got up slowly.

Then she walked to the door and opened it half way.

When the guards came in they pushed the door against the wall. "Rahab, the king sent us. The two men that are here are Israelites. They're here to spy on our city. You must let us bring them to the king."

Rahab looked right into the guards' eyes. She hoped they couldn't tell that her knees were a little shaky. "Yes, there were two men here all right. But I didn't know for sure who they were. In fact, when it was about time to shut the city gate, they left. If you hurry you should be able to catch them. You'd better leave right now, though. If you wait they'll get too far ahead!"

"Thank you, ma'am. We'll be off!" They turned their backs and were gone. Rahab was left standing at the door about to answer them. Her arms flopped to her sides. She could hardly believe she'd gotten rid of the guards so easily.

Quietly she went up to the roof. She tiptoed because she tried not to step on the stalks that once held grain. She had laid them out on the roof to dry. And she was glad she did because that gave her a good place to hide the spies. Next to one big pile she bent over. Carefully she pulled the stalks away until she saw the men. She left them partly covered in case anyone was looking. She pretended to be working with the stalks.

"The guards are gone. We'll have to be careful." Rahab whispered and kept her head down. "I know your God is the true God. We've heard of the great things He does. And I know He's going to give you our city. But promise me one thing, please. Since I've helped you, I'd like you to help me. Save my dad and mom and my brothers and sisters when you take over our city."

"It's a promise, Rahab. But you must not tell anyone about us being here."

"All right then. That's a bargain. I'm going into

the house again. You follow me in a few minutes. Make sure no one sees you."

Rahab went down the steps and into her house. Shortly the spies came too. She told them one more thing to warn them. "Hurry to the mountains. Better hide there three days. Then it'll be safe to go home."

"And now I'll get a rope. You'll have to go out through the window and down the rope. It's a good thing my house is right on the city wall." Carefully and quietly Rahab lowered her guests out of the house.

"Thank you, Rahab. We will be careful. But before we go we want you to take this red cord. Hang it in your window, the one through which you let us down. Then we'll know which house is yours. We promise that no one in this house will be killed. So be sure that your family is with you. We must go now."

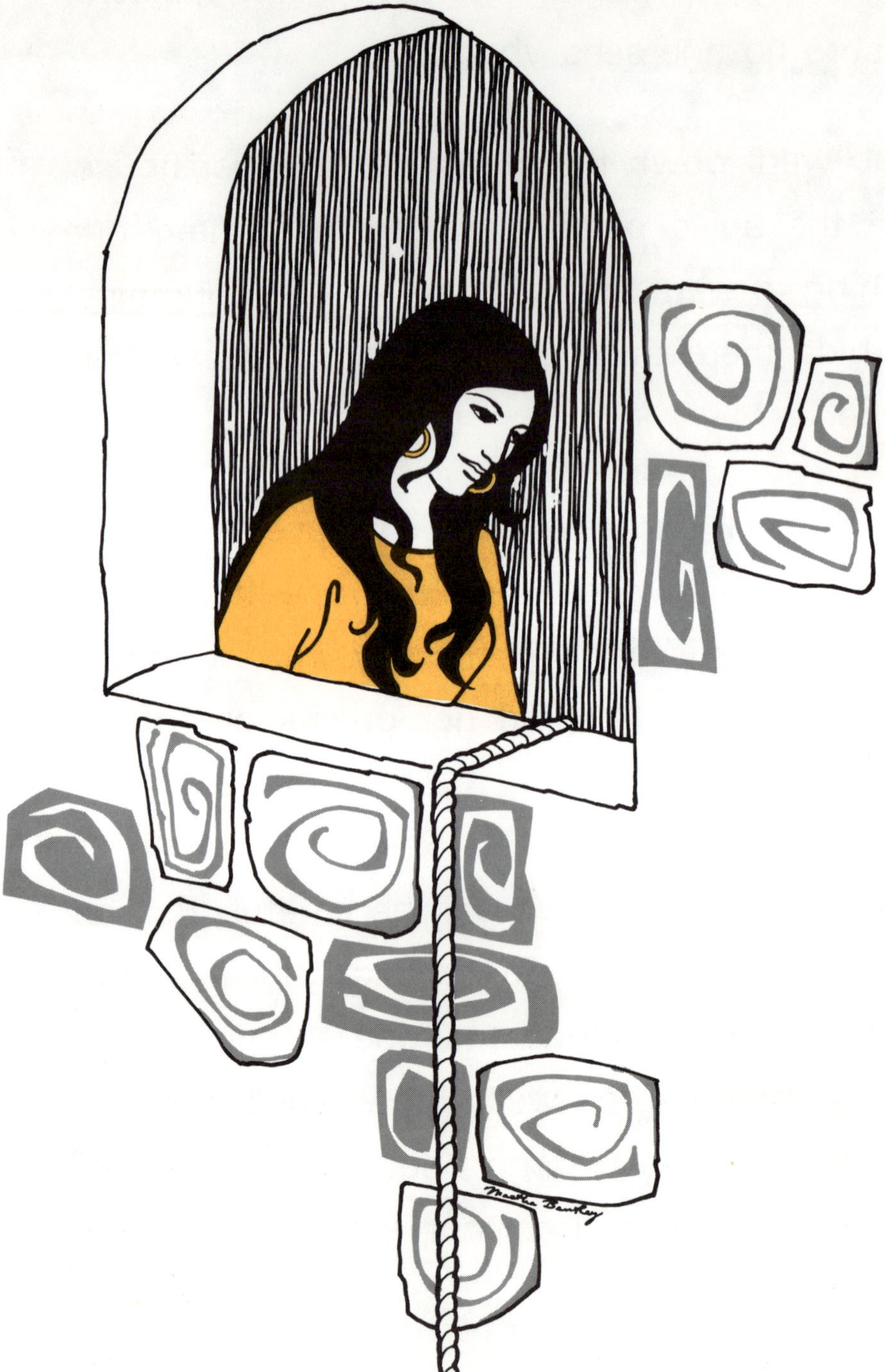

"Just as you say. I'll put the cord in the window now."

Rahab kept the spies in her home because she believed in God. And God kept her safe. Later when the city was taken over, Rahab and her family were safe. They were saved from harm because Rahab had faith.

THE LADY GENERAL

PART ONE

Judges 4:4-9

Israel was in trouble. The people had done it again . . . completely forgot about God. So God let them be conquered by the enemy, King Jabin. Jabin had a general with nine hundred chariots and many more horses. For twenty years Jabin picked fights with the Israelites. He beat them. He did anything he could to be mean. He nearly pestered them to death!

It was Deborah who helped Israel win a battle with Jabin. She was a very busy lady. She had a husband to take care of. She had work to do for God. People came to her to get their squabbles settled. When she talked to them, she also spoke about God. So she always had plenty to do.

One day she called Israel's General Barak to her. She had a special message for him from God. General Barak came in his uniform. He was curious to know why God wanted him.

"General Barak, I'm glad you came. It's good to see you again."

"Glad to see you, Deborah. Is there still more trouble?"

"No, not at all, General. Not if you obey the Lord. He commands you to gather ten thousand men. You are to go to battle against King Jabin's men."

"But, Deborah, that man has all those chariots

and horses besides those strong soldiers, and. . ."

"Listen, General. God will take care of this. He tells you to go to the Kishon River. That's where you will fight. And that's where you will win."

"The Kishon River is all dried up. Hardly a drop of water there right now." He stood up, concerned.

"I know, Barak. But those are your orders!" She turned her back to him.

"All right, Deborah. I'll go. One thing though . . . I'll go only if you come along."

"Me? A lady?"

"Yes, Deborah, only if you come with me."

"Okay, General. I will come. But I'll warn you right now. All the honor for winning this great battle will go to a lady. You won't get any credit for it. How about that!"

"That's all right. I still want you along."

"You'll have to wait while I pack a few things."

Deborah and General Barak went later that day to gather the army.

PART TWO

Judges 4:10-16

General Barak went back home, taking Deborah with him. He sent out word that he needed men. He needed ten thousand men. He wondered how many would come.

Soon they started arriving . . . one hundred from one village. Then came a couple hundred from another. General Barak kept a close count. He had to have ten thousand. When the very last soldier arrived he checked his counting book . . . nine thousand, nine hundred, ninety-nine . . . plus one. That made exactly ten thousand. He had just enough!

He gathered the men together. He gave each one his weapons. Together they went over the battle plans. It was important for each soldier to know the orders. They were going to camp on a mountain. When he was sure that each soldier understood, they were off and marching.

Word spread quickly. King Jabin heard that General Barak was ready to fight. Jabin ordered his general to prepare for battle. Besides all the men, the general also called for his nine hundred chariots. He made sure that his men were ready and waiting to fight at the Kishon River.

Deborah saw the enemy near the river. She called General Barak. "This is the perfect time! The Lord says to go into battle. He is giving you victory!"

General Barak called his men together. It would take them some time to go down the mountain to the river where they would meet the enemy. While the Israelites were getting ready, a few sprinkles fell. As they started out, the rain came faster. The ground started getting slippery and wet. It was harder and harder to walk down the mountain. Water was running down the slopes.

The rushing rain was running straight to the very dry riverbed. River Kishon drank the water as fast as it came. But it wasn't long before there was too much water. Rain was pounding and splattering on the ground. Rain was coming so fast that it filled the riverbed. More rain came. That was followed by still more. Then more. The water ran over the river banks. The water ran crazy and wild. Nothing could stop it!

About the time that General Barak and his men reached the river, the rain was blinding. It flew through the air so fast that people could hardly open their eyes. Their clothes were soggy and dripping. Everything felt soppy and sloshy. The soldiers felt like they weighed a ton. They could barely pick up one leg after another to move.

The water swept over King Jabin's chariots

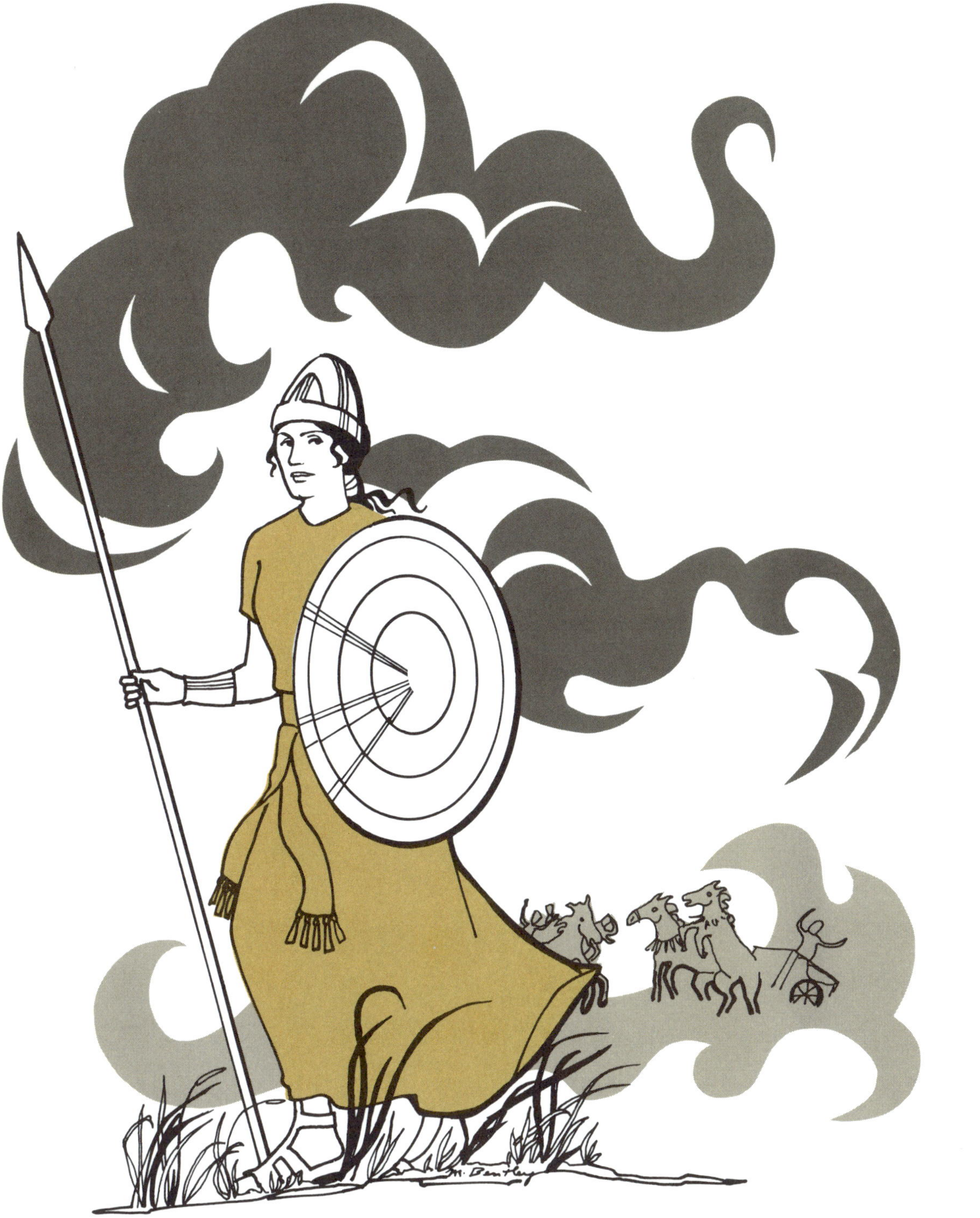

like a giant broom. Such confusion! His men were too upset to think. No one knew what to do or where to run. Their chariots were stuck or lost or broken.

Finally the enemy panicked. They jumped off their horses and chariots and ran. At least they tried to run. It wasn't easy and it wasn't much use. General Barak and his men were right behind them.

In a short time the battle was over. Barak and his men had won. Deborah and Barak sang a song of praise to God.

A PRAYER FOR A BABY

I Samuel 1:5-20

Elkanah had two wives. One had some children. But the other had none. Her name was Hannah. It wasn't that Hannah didn't want children. She loved them very much. It's just that she never became pregnant.

Whenever Elkanah gave out presents, the lady with the children got quite a few. Hannah got only one, but often it was a big one. She had just herself to feed and take care of. How she wished and prayed for a baby boy!

The other lady made it even worse. She teased Hannah. She laughed at her. "Ha-ha! Sure is too bad for you, Hannah."

Hannah turned her head. She didn't want her tears to show. She didn't answer.

"Poor old Hannah. No kids. Now isn't that a shame." She looked at Hannah out of the corner of her eye. She was hoping she had upset her. She enjoyed this mean teasing.

Hannah was upset, very upset. She cried for

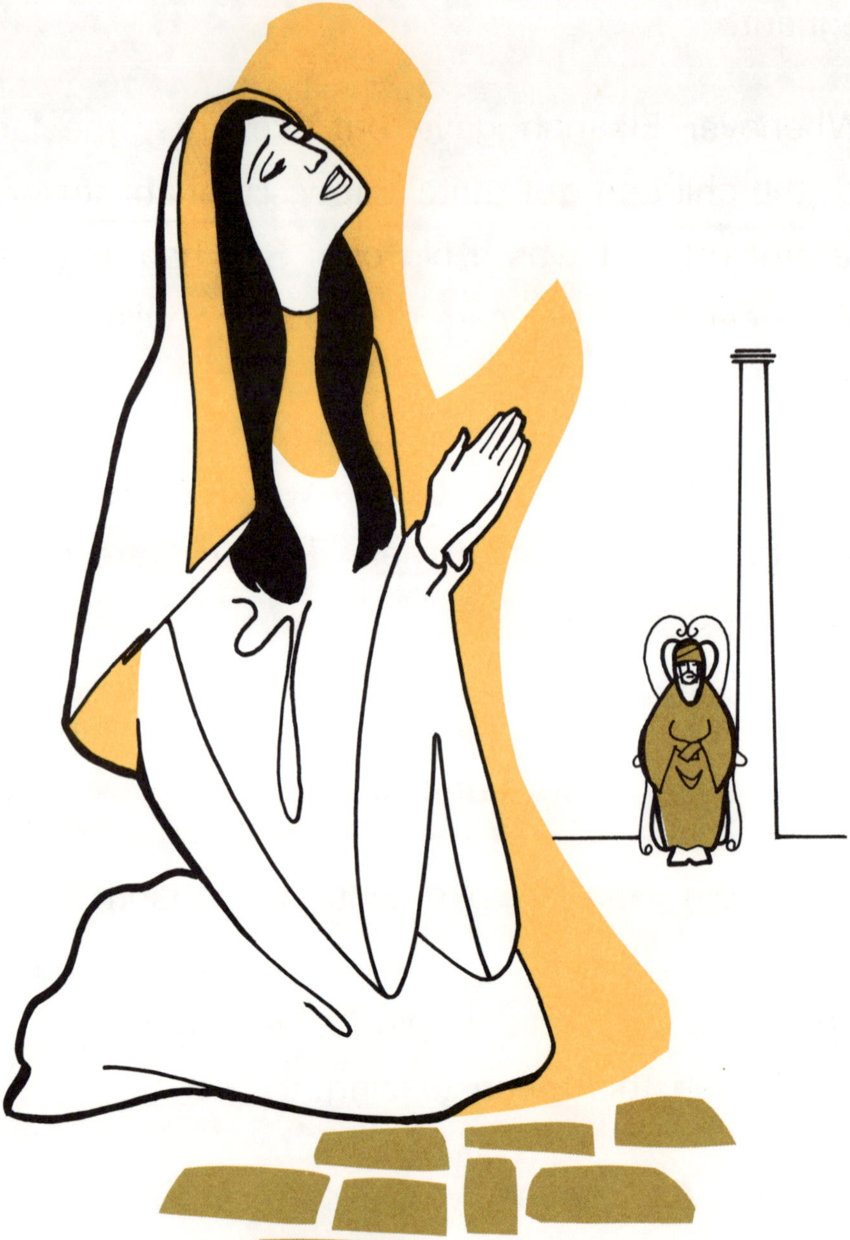

hours. Her eyes were red and puffy. She didn't eat her meals. Her food stayed on the table until it was cold. She sobbed until the tears ran down her face and fell on her plate. How much she hoped for a child!

Sometimes Elkanah became disgusted with his wife. He hated to see her rubbing her swollen red eyes. "Hannah, what's the matter? You haven't even eaten your supper!"

"I-I know it, Elkanah. I just w-wish I could have a baby!"

"Now listen to me. Why make such a fuss over that? You've got me. Isn't that enough? Why, that's even better than ten boys, right?" He waited. She didn't laugh, not even a smile. He could tell that she wasn't in the mood for joking.

Later in the evening Hannah went to the tabernacle. The priest sat by the door. She walked right past him, too upset to notice. She fell on her knees, sobbing quietly as she prayed. Her lips moved. Her body even shook from her silent cries. But she didn't make a sound.

"Dear Lord, please see me and hear me. I'm almost sick from it all. I w-want a baby boy so much. Please, oh, please give me a son. If you do I promise that I will give him b-back to you. You can have him forever, for his whole life!" She stopped to catch some air. Then she continued, under her breath. "To prove my promise, I will never cut his hair, never!"

The priest interrupted her. "Lady, are you drunk? You shouldn't come here like that. This is the tabernacle!" Since her body was shaking and her lips were moving with no sound, he was sure she had had too much wine!

"Oh, no, sir. Please! I'm not drunk. I'm just sad and upset. I was telling my troubles to the Lord. Don't think I'm such a bum. Please don't!"

"Well, that's different then." The priest's face changed quickly from a worried frown to a cheerful smile. "I've got good news. May the Lord give you whatever it is that you want."

"Whatever I want!!

Oh, thank you.

A thousand times, thank you!"

Hannah turned and hurried home. She was hungry again. The lines and puffiness around her eyes disappeared. She didn't need to carry her hanky with her. She wasn't afraid of the teasing. The Lord would give her what she wanted.

About a year later, Hannah had a son. No more teasing. No more sobbing. No more cold food. The Lord gave her a baby boy. She named him Samuel and praised the Lord!

A PLANNED ESCAPE

I Samuel 19:11-17

Carefully I watched the soldiers come toward my house. They were King Saul's men. And I knew just exactly what they came to do. They came to kill my husband. That wasn't very hard to figure out. King Saul had tried to kill David before. In fact, just a few hours ago the king threw a spear at him. He tried to pin David to the wall. But David jumped up quickly enough to get away.

That's why I worried. These men stayed close to our house. They were snooping around. And I knew that meant only one thing. King Saul was going to try again to kill David. Only this time he was sending his soldiers to do it for him.

I knew I had to do something. I was ready to do almost anything to save David's life. So I came right out and told him, hoping no one was listening. "David, our house is being watched. King Saul's men are all over. If you want to stay alive, you'd better get out tonight. If you wait 'til tomorrow, you'll be dead."

"But, Michal, that's almost impossible. How could I sneak away now?"

"I have a plan. It'll be hard. But we've got to try it. It's the only way I can think of saving you. You'll have to get a rope and I'll let you down through the window. I'll take care of everything else. Don't worry."

"All right, Michal. You're right. I'd better hurry. There's no time to waste. Be right back with the rope."

When David got back, I let him out the small window at the back of the house. He was very heavy. I held on so tightly that I got blisters on my hands. At last he touched the ground. I saw him disappear around the corner of the house. Then I hurried to the living room. We have a statue that's about the size of a person. I dragged it all the way to the bedroom. Then I tipped it up onto the bed. I laid it on a pillow made of goat's hair. After I tucked it in, it looked like a real man. It would fool anyone.

In the morning I heard a knock on the door. "Yes," I answered. "Who is it?"

"King Saul's men. We would like to see David."

I opened the door. "I'm sorry. David is sick." Then I closed the door.

Later the men came again. "The King wants to see David anyway. We'll carry him to the palace on his bed. Where is he?"

"In the bedroom . . . that way." I pointed to the door and waited.

When they came out of the room, they were angry. They had seen my trick. It was only a statue in the bed. The men were grumbling and mumbling as they left.

In a short time King Saul himself was at my house. "Michal," he hollered. "Why, just why, did you let David get away?"

"I had to, King Saul. David said that he would kill me if I didn't help him get away."

King Saul was furious with me. But I didn't care. I loved David. I knew that somewhere David, dear David, was hiding and safe.

A FEAST IN THE WILDERNESS

I Samuel 25:3-35

David and his many men were hiding in very hilly and rocky country. They lived among the sheep . . . three thousand of them! These sheep didn't belong to them, though. They belonged to a very rich man named Nabal. His wife's name was Abigail.

There were many times that David and his helpers were hungry. But they never killed a lamb, not once. In fact, they protected the sheep and the shepherds. They were a big help to Nabal.

One day David called ten of his men together. "Go, visit our friend, Nabal. Say hello to him for me. I hope all is well with his home and everything he owns. Ask him if he is willing to give us a gift. Maybe something to eat. We would appreciate it."

The young men came to Nabal's sheep ranch. They gave Nabal the message from David. But Nabal wasn't at all nice about it. "David? Who is he? Why should I take the food from my own men and give it to him? Just who does this David think he is? No, sir. I will give him nothing. Not one thing!"

When David's men came back with the message, David picked up his sword. As he strapped it on, he gave orders to the others. "All right, men.

Grab your swords. We will have to get ready to fight. What a foolish man that Nabal is."

While this was happening, one of Nabal's men told Abigail that her husband had been very unkind. Abigail felt very badly. She knew that David was God's servant. How she wished her husband wasn't so stubborn and cocky. She decided to do something about it herself.

Abigail ordered the servants to bring the donkeys near the house. On one donkey she put two barrels of rich sweet wine. One barrel was strapped to each side of the animal. On the second she put two bushels of roasted grain, dry and tasty. On the next few donkeys she put two hundred loaves of freshly baked bread. Then she loaded one hundred bunches of raisins on the next donkeys. She wrapped five whole sheep, killed and ready for roasting. These were loaded on the other donkeys. On the very last donkey, she packed two hundred fig cakes. The cakes were made from dried figs and were full of this chewy rich fruit. Then she started out, taking this feast to David.

David saw Abigail coming. He was surprised with such delicious-looking food. They hadn't seen food like this in weeks!

Abigail quickly got off her donkey and bowed low in front of David. "Forgive my foolish husband. He has such a temper. Here you were so good to him and our shepherds. I'm very sorry this happened. The Lord will reward you for your goodness."

"Why thank you, Abigail. And thank the Lord for sending you. If you hadn't come, we would have killed your husband and his men. But don't worry now, Abigail. Go on home. Your life is safe and so is your husband's."

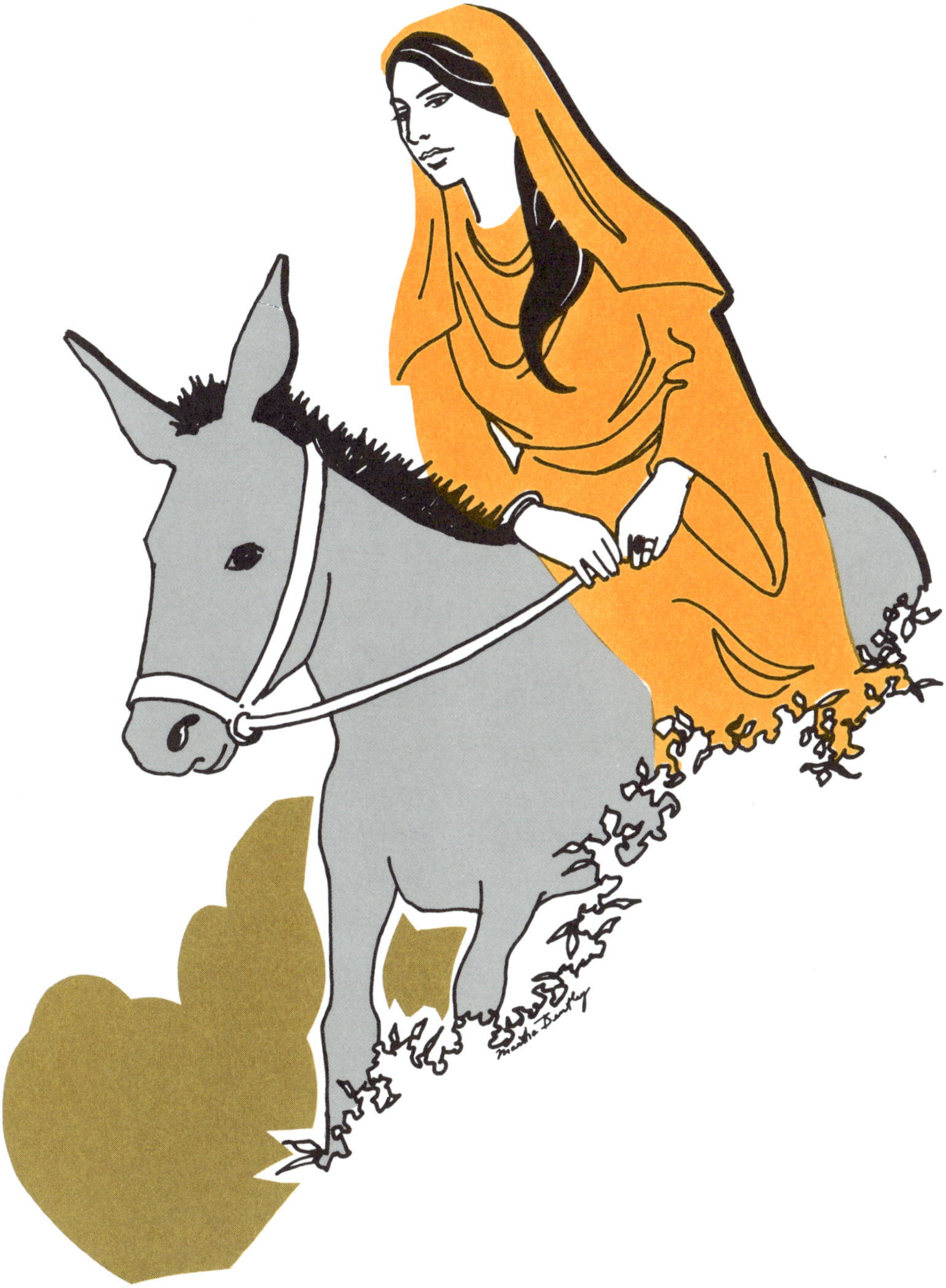

BREAD FOR TOMORROW

I Kings 17:8-17

NARRATOR: The Lord always took care of Elijah, the prophet. Sometimes God sent birds to bring him meat and bread. He drank water from a brook. When the brook dried up, the Lord told him to go to Zarephath. A widow who lived there would take care of him. When Elijah arrived, he saw a lady picking up sticks.

ELIJAH: Pardon me, ma'am. Will you get me a cup of water?

LADY: I'd be happy to. It'll take me just a minute. Be right back.

ELIJAH: Say, while you're getting that, bring along a slice of bread.

LADY: (turning back toward Elijah) I'm

terribly sorry. I don't have a slice of bread to give you. All I have is a little bit of flour. Not more than a handful. I guess there is a bit of oil left too. I was just getting some sticks together. Thought I'd build a fire, then bake some bread for my son and me. That'll about take care of our last little bit of food.

ELIJAH: Then what?

LADY: I guess my son and I will starve to death.

ELIJAH: Please don't worry about starving. Go right ahead and use that flour. But bake a little loaf for me first. Then there will still be enough for you and your boy.

LADY: But there's such a little.

ELIJAH: The Lord says there will always

be just enough flour left. At least until the crops grow again.

LADY: I will do as you say, Elijah.

NARRATOR: Quickly the lady built a fire. She mixed the flour and oil together and added a few other things. One small loaf was for Elijah. The other one was for herself and her son. It smelled so good while it baked. It looked crusty and brown. The lady looked back into her flour jar. There was plenty for tomorrow, just as the Lord had said.

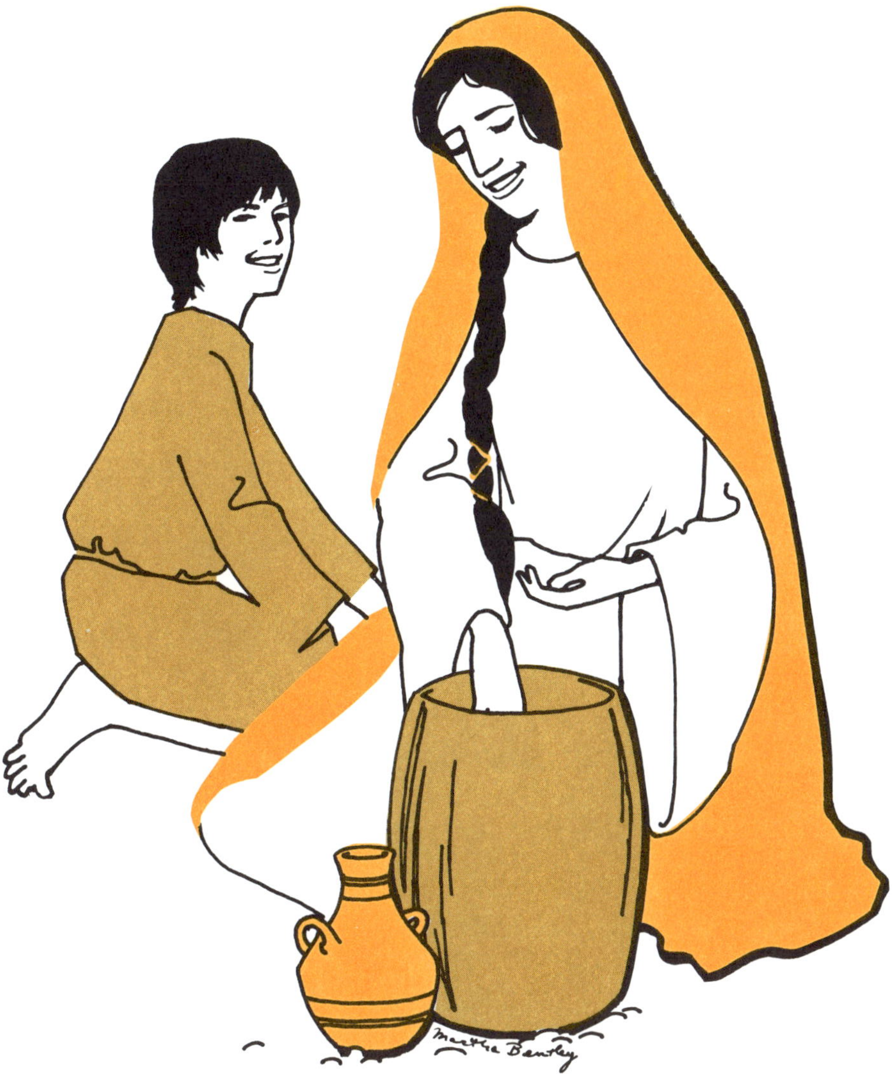
Martha Bentley

JARS AND POTS ALL OVER

II Kings 4:1-7

Mrs. Obadiah was frantic. She didn't have any money. Her cupboards were empty . . . no cereal, no bread, not even a cracker. Her two boys were hungry and so was she. But what worried her most was the bill collector. He came to her house quite often. And the last time he came, he had terrible news. If she didn't pay her bills pretty soon, he was going to take her two boys as slaves. The thought was more than she could stand.

That's why she came to see Elisha, God's prophet. She told him the whole story. Elisha could see how upset she was. Her husband was dead. She had no money, none at all. And now she probably would have to lose her boys.

"All right, Mrs. Obadiah. Let's see what can be done. Just exactly how much food do you have in your house right now?"

"I don't have a thing! Nothing except one jar of olive oil." She looked down at the floor and slowly shook her head. Everything seemed so hopeless.

"You can get started right now," Elisha told her. "Begin borrowing some jars and pots. Go to your friends and your relatives. Stop in at your neighbors. Get just as many jars as you can find and take them home with you. Then go inside. Take your boys and the jars with you. After you shut the door, start pouring oil from your little jar. Just keep on pouring. When one jar is full, get the next one."

Mrs. Obadiah was excited about the plan. She did just what Elisha told her to do. She had big jars, little jars, tall round jars, short fat pots, and pots in all different colors. When she had the jars and pots and her boys in the house, she shut the door.

Reaching to the top shelf, she got the jar of olive oil. It was just a little jar. But she was thankful for it. How careful she was not to drop it. Slowly she tipped it, pouring oil into one of the big pots. Oil kept pouring out of that tiny jar. It filled one big pot, then another and another and another. Her boys kept bringing empty jars and pots. And all this time, the little jar of olive oil kept filling them.

When one jar was about full, she called to her sons. "Hurry now! Bring me another empty one."

"But, mom, there aren't any more. They're all full."

She set the little jar down. It was empty. She tipped it again, but no more oil came out. The little jar had filled every one of the jars and pots!

Mrs. Obadiah was quite excited. She ran to tell God's servant. "They're full, Elisha. Every jar and pot I could find is full of olive oil."

"Now you must sell the oil, Mrs. Obadiah. Take it

with you to the market. Then pay all your bills. You will have enough money left to live on for the rest of your life."

Elisha was right. Mrs. Obadiah's sons were able to stay right at home. And her purse was never empty again!

A SURPRISE GIFT TWICE

PART ONE

II Kings 4:8-17

Elisha stopped to have supper with some friends of his. They were a special man and lady to him. He knew he would always have a delicious meal at their house. They would also have a place for him and his servant, Gehazi, to stay.

These people liked Elisha a lot, too. They did everything they could to help. Just for him they built an extra bedroom up on their roof. This way

Elisha had a place to stay when he was in town. He could be by himself a little bit. The room had everything he needed. Besides a bed and a chair, there was a table and lamp. Elisha could read and study. And it was quiet up there. He could be alone with God in prayer.

One day while Elisha was resting he called his servant. "Tell the lady I'd like to talk with her." Gehazi hurried downstairs to get her.

When she came Elisha spoke. "You have been so kind to us. We'd like to do something for you. Would it help if we told the king how good you are? Or maybe we should tell the captain?"

"Not really," she answered. "I'm quite happy. There's not a thing I need." Then she turned and went back downstairs.

Later Elisha asked Gehazi, "Just what can we do for that lady? There must be something."

"Well, maybe there is one thing. She doesn't

have a son. Her husband is such an old man. She probably never will have a little boy. That is not unless God . . . "

"That's it, Gehazi! What a beautiful idea for a present. Ask her to come up again."

Gehazi hurried down the steps. He was eager to hear Elisha tell her about the surprise gift that God would give her.

When she came back, she stood in the doorway. Elisha spoke first. "Next year about this time you will have a baby boy!"

"Oh, Elisha. Don't be silly. That can't be. You know you shouldn't lie to me about something special like that. I must go now. Good-bye."

The lady closed the door softly. She smiled about their talk. What an impossible idea, she thought. She knew that Elisha was God's prophet. She should have known that God keeps his promises. A year later she had a baby. It was a

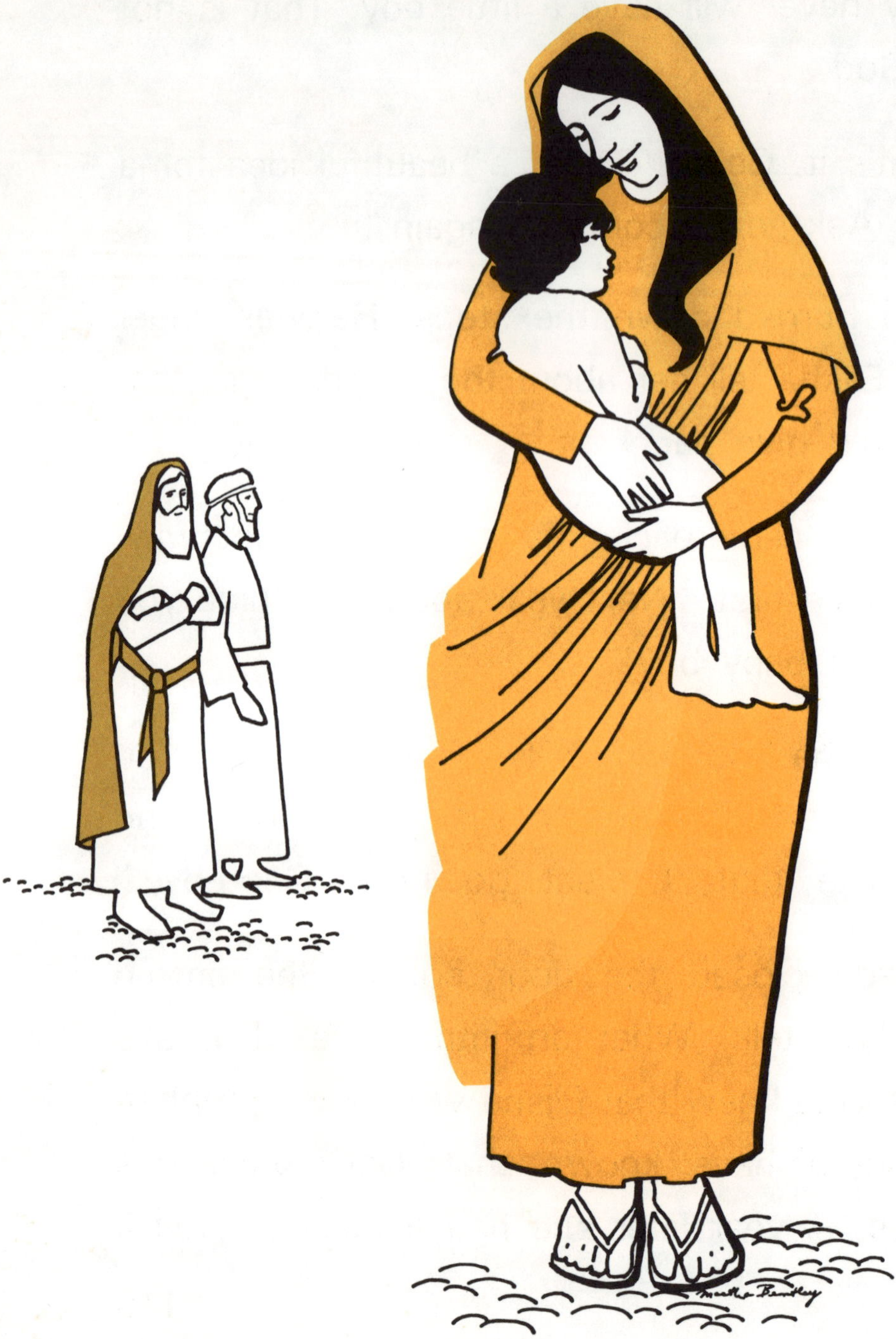

boy just as Elisha had said it would be. Now God's promise was not only in her mind, not only in her heart. She held God's precious promise in her arms! God gave her a baby.

PART TWO

II Kings 4:18-37

One day the boy went out to help his dad. He was a little older now. He had such a headache. He cried to his father. "Dad, I don't feel very well! I've got an awful pain in my head."

Father looked at him. The boy was lying on the ground. He rolled from side to side. He was crying and holding his head. "Quickly, my servant!" he hollered. "Get this boy home to his mother. Don't waste a minute."

When the boy was brought home, the lady put the boy in her lap. She snuggled him close to her.

He was her only son. How much she loved him. But she couldn't help him. About lunchtime he died in her lap.

Tenderly she carried his little body up to the roof. She put him on the bed in Elisha's room. Then she left, quietly and sadly. She shut the door behind her.

Immediately she sent for a servant. She told him to bring a donkey. The animal he chose had to be strong. The trip she was planning to take would be about twenty-five miles. When they came she put the saddle on the donkey. While she climbed up, she gave orders to the servant. "Now I want you to hurry. We're going to see Elisha. Keep this donkey walking just as fast as it will go. Pull it along if you have to. Don't slow down or stop for anything unless I tell you to."

When they came to the mountain she saw Elisha near the top. She could hear him calling.

"Gehazi, look! It's our friend. Run out and say hello. Find out if something's wrong. Maybe it's her husband . . . or it could be her little boy. Quickly, Gehazi."

As Gehazi came to her, she told him that things were okay. She didn't want to waste time. She wanted to talk with Elisha.

When the donkey stopped in front of Elisha, she jumped off, tired from the long ride. She threw herself down on the ground. She grabbed at Elisha's feet. Gehazi started to push her away. But Elisha stopped him. "No, Gehazi. Something's wrong. The Lord hasn't told me about it. So let her speak."

She talked quickly, angrily. "Elisha, you're the one who said I'd have a son. Then you asked God to give him to me. I begged you not to lie to me . . ."

Elisha stopped her. "Gehazi, hurry to the lady's

house. Take my cane. Lay it on the boy's face. Don't stop to talk with anyone!"

"Listen to me, Elisha. I'm not going home without you. I won't move unless you come too!"

"All right. I'll come. But you, Gehazi, run on ahead of us. And remember what I told you to do."

Gehazi hurried. He never went so fast in his life. When he got to the lady's house, he flew up the steps, two at a time. He laid Elisha's cane on the boy's face. But nothing happened . . . nothing!

When Elisha got there the child was still dead. He went into the room and closed the door. He got down on his knees and prayed to God. Then he laid down on the little boy. The body was stiff and cold.

Carefully Elisha put his big hands on the boy's little fingers and hands. He put his eyes on top of the closed eyes of the boy. Then he put his mouth over the boy's mouth. Elisha felt that cold little body slowly getting warm, then warmer and warmer.

Elisha got up and went downstairs. He walked back and forth in the house a few times. Then he went back upstairs. Slowly he laid on the boy just as before.

Suddenly the boy took a deep breath and went Ah-ah-ah-choo!! One, two, three times, four, five, six, seven loud sneezes! He opened his eyes. They were a lively dark brown.

When the lady was called she hurried into the room. She fell to the floor, so thankful. Then she stood up and took hold of her son. She held him tightly. It was great for her to hold his warm and wiggly body again. God had given her this precious boy not once, but twice!

AN ANGEL VISIT

Luke 1:26-38

NARRATOR: God sent the angel Gabriel to visit Mary. He is bringing her a very important message from God.

GABRIEL: Congratulations, Mary! You are a very special lady. God is with you.

MARY: What? Special? (Mary mumbles to herself. She is confused, even a little scared.) Why are you here, angel?

GABRIEL: Please don't be afraid, Mary. God is going to bless you more than any other lady. You are going to have a baby. It'll be a little boy. When He is born you must name Him Jesus.

MARY: Yes, go on. Please tell me more.

GABRIEL: He will be the most important baby

ever born. In fact, He will be the Son of God! He will be a King. Not just any old king. He'll be a King who will live and rule forever and ever.

MARY: Just a minute, though. I guess I don't understand how that can be. I don't even know anyone who could be the baby's father. Please explain it more.

GABRIEL: That's just it, Mary. This baby won't have a real father on this earth. This baby will be God's Son. God will be His Father.

MARY: I do believe in God. If He wants me to have this baby, I will. Everything God promises comes true.

GABRIEL: I must be going now.

NARRATOR: Mary believed the angel. She knew

that she was truly going to be the mother of Jesus. Soon she and Joseph would be married. But Joseph wouldn't be His real Father. Joseph would adopt Jesus, to help take care of Him while He lived on earth.

PRAISING GOD AT EIGHTY-FOUR

Luke 2:36-40

Anna got up slowly. Her knees were getting sore. Her joints felt just a little stiff. Sometimes it was hard for her to kneel for praying. She remembered how easily she used to get around. But now she was eighty-four. She had to be quite careful as she worked in the temple. Yet she was thankful even though she was old. She could still fold her thin and wrinkled hands in prayer. She loved the Lord so much.

One of the things Anna often prayed for was the

coming of Christ. Long, long ago God had promised to send the Savior. People waited for Him. They were eager and anxious. It was like waiting for a most wonderful and unusual present. That's why people who believed in God often prayed that He would send His Son soon. They hoped to see Him, to listen to Him, even to touch Him. Anna, too, waited for baby Jesus.

On this particular day Anna wasn't alone in the temple. She was with Simeon, an old, old man. She heard him talking to someone. She looked in. She saw that he was talking to Joseph and Mary. They were Jesus' father and mother. Anna watched. Simeon was holding the little baby. His face glowed like a candle. He was thanking God. He had lived to see the little Christ-child, the Savior!

Anna hurried into the room. For a minute she forgot about her eighty-four-year-old body. She was thinking about only one thing . . . seeing Jesus, precious baby Jesus.

As she looked at this little child, she nearly burst with joy. Anna threw her arms in the air. She wanted to cry and laugh. Her face and lips were lined and wrinkled. But she spoke clearly and beautifully. "Thank you, Lord! I'm so happy that I lived to see this little child. You have sent the Savior, just as You promised. Thank you for Your goodness."

Then Anna left the temple. To everyone that asked about the Savior, Anna answered quickly. "I have seen Him. The Lord has sent His Son. Christ, the Savior is born!"

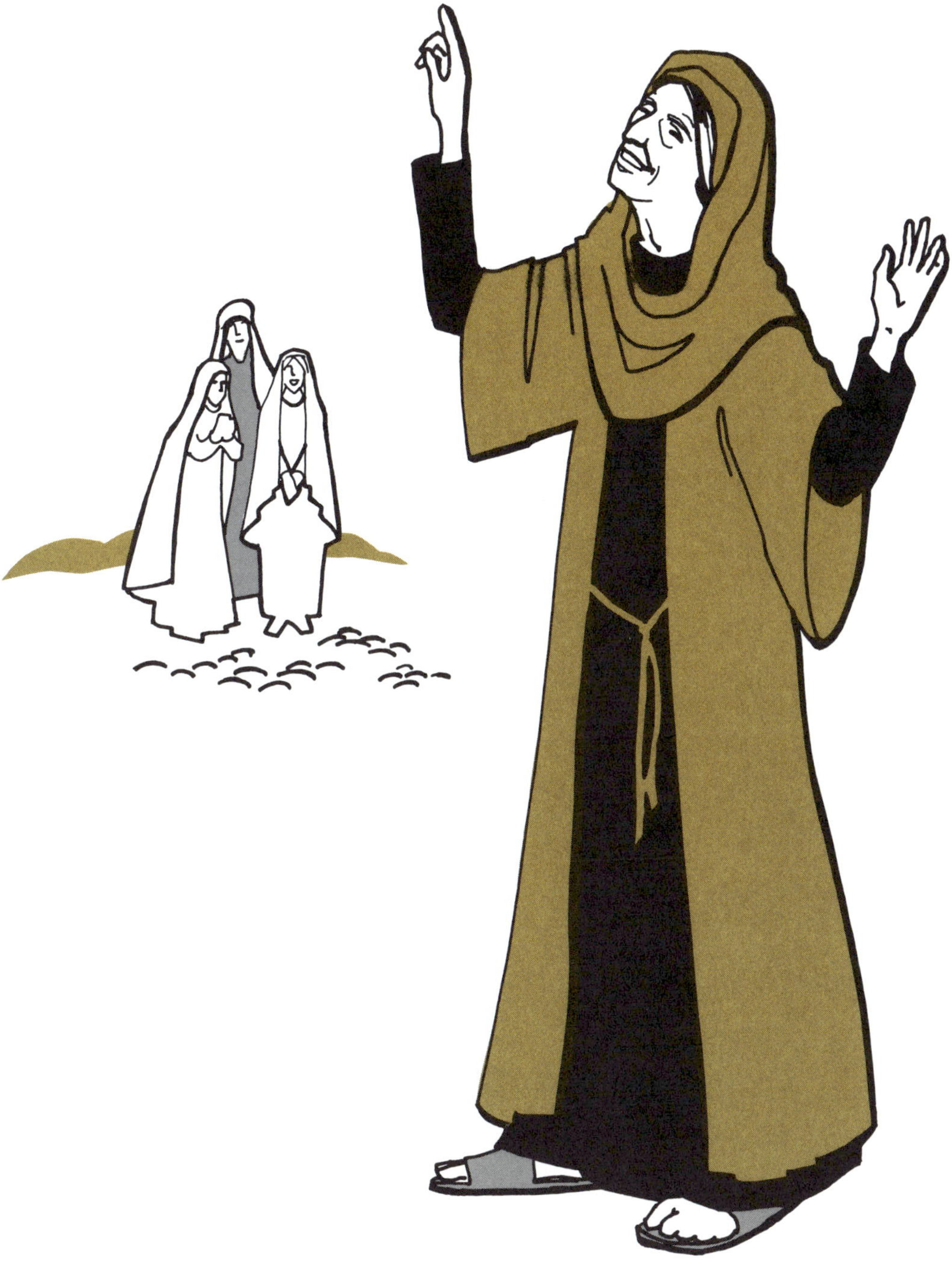

PRAISE GOD, I AM HEALED!

Mark 5:25-34

I was known around town as unclean;
So I lived trying not to be seen.
How I wished I could be healed!

I'd been bleeding for so many years
When I heard that the Lord would be here;
So I hurried to be healed!

I came to the crowd almost sneaking,
Pushing my way without speaking.
I knew I'd soon be healed!

I bent on my knees in the street
Though all I could see was His feet.
Surely I'd be healed!

I touched just the hem of His clothing
When I felt that the blood had stopped flowing.
Just like that—I was healed!

He asked who had given that touch,
But no one could tell very much.
So many had come to be healed!

He knew in exactly that hour
That He had been using His power.
Someone had been healed!

Frightened by what I had done,
I admitted, "Lord, I'm the one.
How I wanted to be healed!"

He told me that I could go home.
I was healed by my faith alone.
Praise the Lord, I am healed!

A RHYTHM STORY — rhythm stories are explained on page 10.

WHO GAVE MORE?

Mark 12:41-44

The	Lord	sat	in	the	tem-	ple	
And	watched	the	folks	who	passed.		
Some	of	them	came	right	in-	side	
To	bring	their	gifts	of	cash.		
Cer-	tain	men	walked	to	the	box,	
Their	clothes	were	cleaned	and	pressed;		
Their	suits	were	made	of	col-	ored	silk
They	were	the	ver-	y	best!		
The	men	gave	lots	of	mon-	ey,	
They	brought	it	up	in	bags.		
Then	came	a	poor,	poor	la-	dy,	
Her	clothes	were	more	like	rags.		
She	dropped	in	a	cou-	ple	coins	
Worth	a-	bout	a	pen-	ny.		
The	wealth-	y	men	had	more	at	home
But	she	had	not	left	an-	y.	

130

The	Lord	saw	what	had	hap-	pened	
And	asked	who'd	giv-	en	more.		
It	was	the	one	who	gave	it	all...
The	la-	dy,	old	and	poor.		

A GIFT AT THE WELL

John 4:4-42

NARRATOR: It was almost time for lunch. Jesus and the disciples had been walking quite awhile. They were tired and hot. Since they had no food, the disciples went to buy groceries. Jesus sat alone by the well and waited. Along came a lady from Samaria to get water.

JESUS: Pardon me, ma'am. May I have a drink of water?

LADY: Certainly, sir. Just a minute. (She pulled up her water jar and poured some for Jesus.)

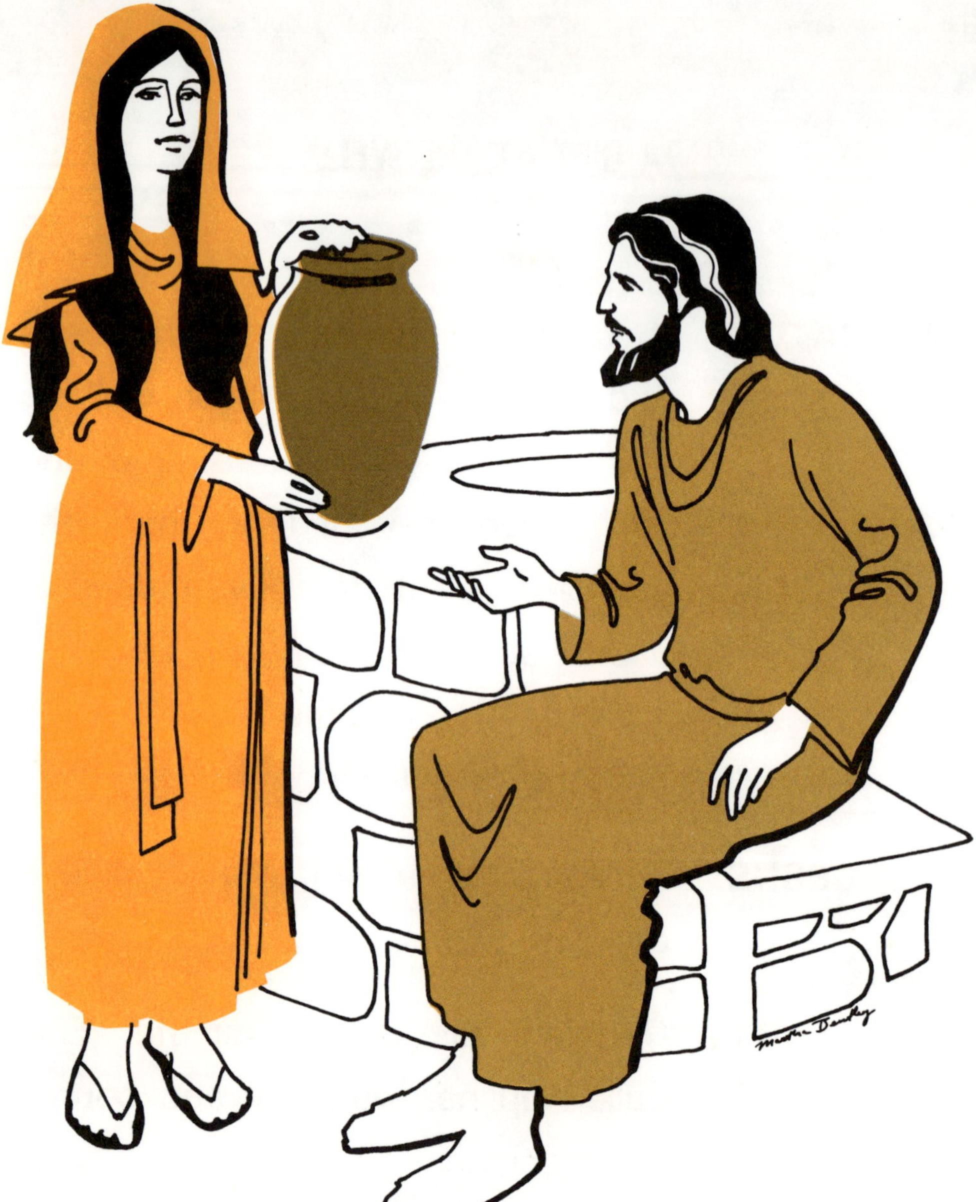

JESUS: Thank you so much. (He drank it quickly.)

LADY: You're welcome. I'm a little surprised that you asked. You people don't usually even speak to us Samaritans.

JESUS: Perhaps. But if you knew who I am and what I can give you, you would have asked me for some living water.

LADY: (smiling to herself) But that would be silly. You don't even have a water jar with you. Besides you forgot your rope! This well is pretty deep.

JESUS: Yes, I know.

LADY: But wait, where would you get this special living water? This well is Jacob's. Can your water be better than this?

JESUS: Much better! You see, when you drink water from this well, you'll soon be thirsty again. The water I can give you lasts forever and ever!

LADY: Please, sir. Give me some of that water. Then I'll never be thirsty again. Just think of it. Never again will I have to make this long trip with my rope and water jar.

JESUS: (changing the subject) Go and get your husband.

LADY: Well, I can't. Not now. (She turned away from Him. She was blushing.) I'm not married.

JESUS: (He could see that she was embarrassed.) Yes, I know that. You have already had five husbands. Besides that you're living with another man right now. He's not even your husband.

LADY: Sir, you must be a prophet. You seem to know everything.

NARRATOR: The lady tried to change the subject again. She talked about God and where to worship.

LADY: Oh, well, the Messiah will come. You know who I mean, the Christ. He'll explain all my questions about God.

JESUS: I am the Christ.

NARRATOR: At that moment, the disciples came back with the groceries. The lady left. She hurried home, calling her friends.

LADY: You must come quickly. Christ is here! He told me everything that I ever did. Hurry! He's at the well now. If you come right away you can talk with Him yourselves.

NARRATOR: The city folks hurried to see Jesus. Many of them believed and asked for living water. Jesus gave it freely to each one who asked. He gave them the promise of living forever with God!

JESUS GAVE HER WATER

Arranged by Alfred B. Smith

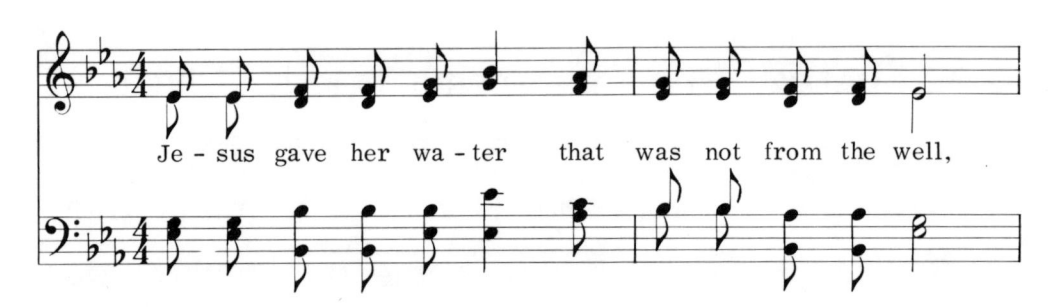

Je - sus gave her wa - ter that was not from the well,

©1942 by Singspiration, Inc. All rights reserved. Used by permission.

Gave her living water and sent her forth to tell; She went away singing, And came back bringing Others for the water that was not from the well.

A RHYTHM STORY — rhythm stories are explained on page 10.

A FOOT BATH

John 12:1-8

Ma-	ry	bought	a	spe-	cial	gift	
To	give	to	Christ	some	day,		
It	was	a	jar	of	rich	per-	fume,
It	cost	a	whole	year's	pay.		
One	eve-	ning	at	a	par-	ty	
She	saw	the	guests	ar-	rive,		
She	watched	where	Je-	sus	went	to	sit,
Then	sat	down	by	His	side.		
She	took	the	jar	of	rich	per-	fume
And	poured	it	on	His	feet.		

The fragrance went throughout the house,
It smelled so rich and sweet.

The people there were quite surprised
But Mary didn't care.
She bent down by Jesus' feet
And wiped them with her hair.

Judas thought that she was dumb
To waste away her pay.
But Jesus thought it was all right.
She showed her love that way.

(softly)
She showed her love that way.

MARY!

John 1:1-16

I had seen how Christ died on the cross,
I felt such a great, empty loss—
He was my friend and my Savior, my Lord!

I hurried to visit His tomb,
Taking spices that smelled of perfume—
At least I could look at my Lord!

I arrived very early that day,
And found that huge stone rolled away—
Oh, where have they taken my Lord!

Two angels were sitting inside,
They asked, "Tell us, why do you cry?"
I answered, "They've t-taken my Lord!"

I wept. Yes, I sobbed as I cried.
While a man stepped up close to my side—
Perhaps it is he who has taken my Lord!

Before I was ready to speak,
He asked quietly, "Why do you weep"?
"B-because, sir, they've stolen my Lord!"

"Oh, sir, I have something to say,
Have you put my Lord's body away?
Don't you see, sir? He was my Lord!"

"Mary!" He said just that word,
I could hardly believe what I'd heard—
It was the voice of my Savior, my Lord!

I cried out with joy and relief,
Gone were my fears and my grief—
"Oh, Master! My Savior! My Lord!"

WE WELCOME GLAD EASTER

ST. DENIO

Welsh Hymn Melody, c. 1839

1 We welcome glad Easter when Jesus arose
2 And tell how the women came early that day

And won a great victory over His foes.
And there at the tomb found the stone rolled away.

REFRAIN

Then raise your glad voices, ye children, and sing;

Bring sweet East-er prais-es to Je-sus our King.

3 And sing of the angel who said, "Do not fear!
   Your Savior is ris'n again; He is not here."

4 And think of the promise which Jesus did give:
   "That he who believes in Me also shall live!"

Author Unknown

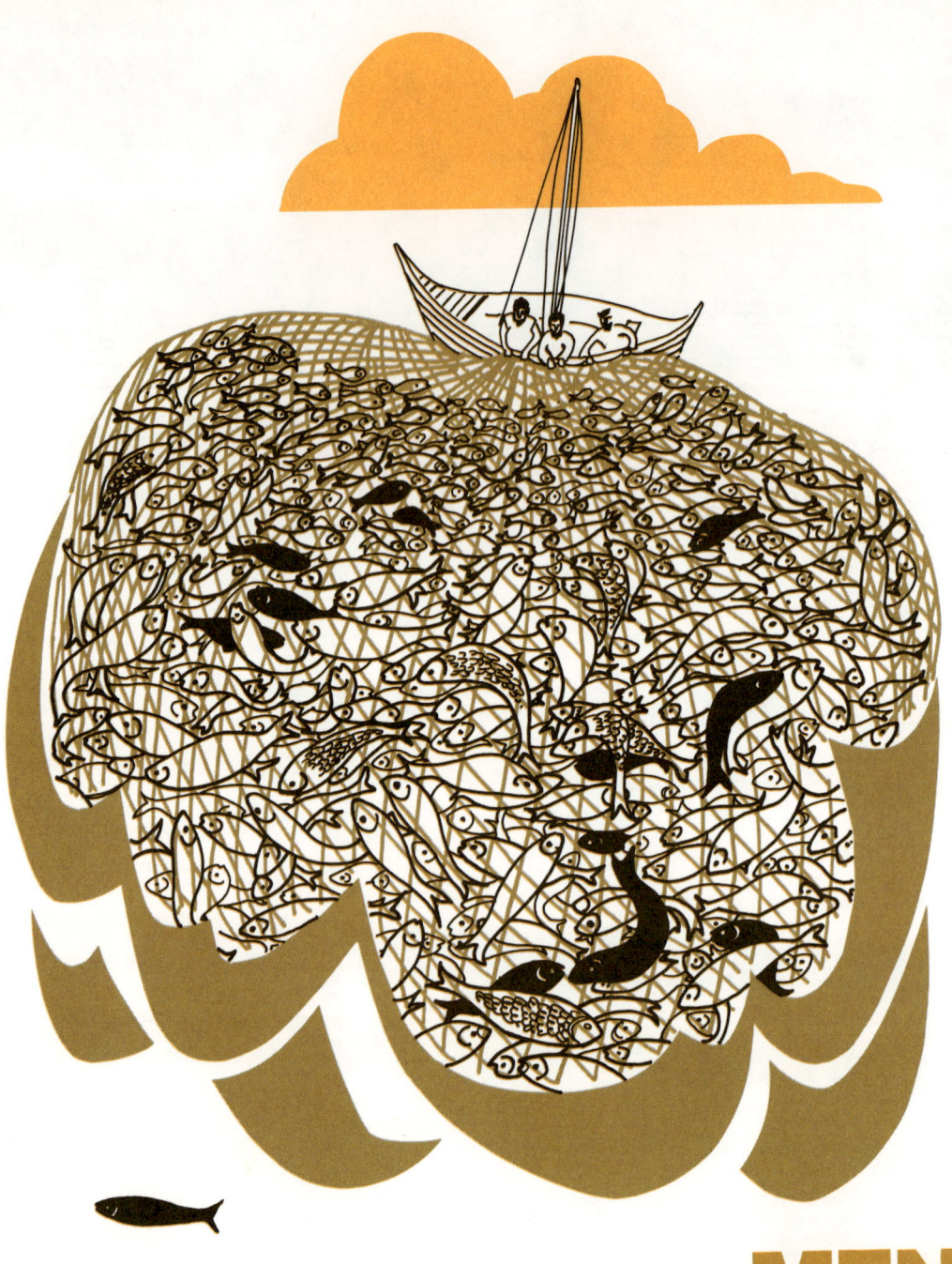

MEN

The Time the World Drowned	146
Kiss and Make Up	148
Rags to Riches	153
The City that Crashed	164
The Mightiest Man	166
Whirlwind to Heaven	175
Rescue by Rope	179
A Strange Place to Spend the Night	185
John the Baptizer	188
The Graveyard Monster	192
The Bold Fisherman	197
Song: I Will Make You Fishers of Men	202
The Plan that Healed a Friend	214
Song: Ten Lepers	216
Just One Came Back	218
Song: Zaccheus	220
A One O'clock Miracle	223
Death of a Friend	227
Just in Time	229
Empty Chains	231
Earthquake at Midnight	235

OF THE BIBLE

A RHYTHM STORY — rhythm stories are explained on page 10.

THE TIME THE WORLD DROWNED

Genesis 6—9

God's	world	be-	came	so	sin-	ful,	
It	made	the	Lord	quite	sad;		
Be-	cause	the	peo-	ple	He	had	made,
Were	act-	ing	ver-	y	bad.		
God	came	to	talk	to	No-	ah,	
Told	him	to	build	a	boat,		
"I	want	it	made	quite	care-	ful-	ly.
Be	cer-	tain	that	it	floats!"		
No-	ah	worked	for	months	and	years	
And	when	it	all	was	done,		
He	called	all	the	liv-	ing	things,	
Took	some	of	ev-	ery	one.		

When Noah and his folks were in,
God came and closed the door.
He started all the floods and rain,
Oh! how it did pour!

Forty days and nights it rained.
The wicked were all drowned.
But on the inside of the boat
All was safe and sound.

Soon God dried His soppy world,
Then opened up the door,
He promised Noah and his folks
To bless them evermore!

(softly)
And drown the world no more!
And drown the world no more!

147

KISS AND MAKE UP

Genesis 32 — 33

Jacob and Esau hadn't seen each other in years, not since Jacob pulled a mean trick on Esau. By fooling their blind old father, Jacob had gotten the special blessing that belonged to Esau. Jacob's trick made Esau so angry that he said he'd kill Jacob. Jacob was afraid and quickly left home before Esau got a chance to kill him.

Now, years later, Jacob wanted to visit his brother. But he didn't feel sure about doing it. He had no way of knowing whether Esau still hated him. So he sent a message. It read:

Hello from Jacob!

I have been living with our Uncle Laban for a long time. It was just a little while ago that I moved away. Now I am fairly rich. I own oxen, donkeys, sheep, and servants. I'm sending these messengers to tell you that we're coming to visit. I sure hope you will be nice to us.

*Your brother,
Jacob*

When the messengers returned, they told Jacob that Esau was coming to meet him . . . with an army of four hundred men! Jacob panicked! Four hundred men? Already on their way? Oh, no! My wives! My kids! What'll I do? There was no question about it. Jacob was scared stiff!

Just as soon as Jacob could think a little straight, he divided everything into two groups . . . oxen, donkeys, sheep, and servants. He figured that if Esau attacked one group, the other might be able to get away. Then, when that big job was finished, Jacob prayed to God for safety.

It was almost dark when Jacob gathered a present for Esau. It was quite a gift!

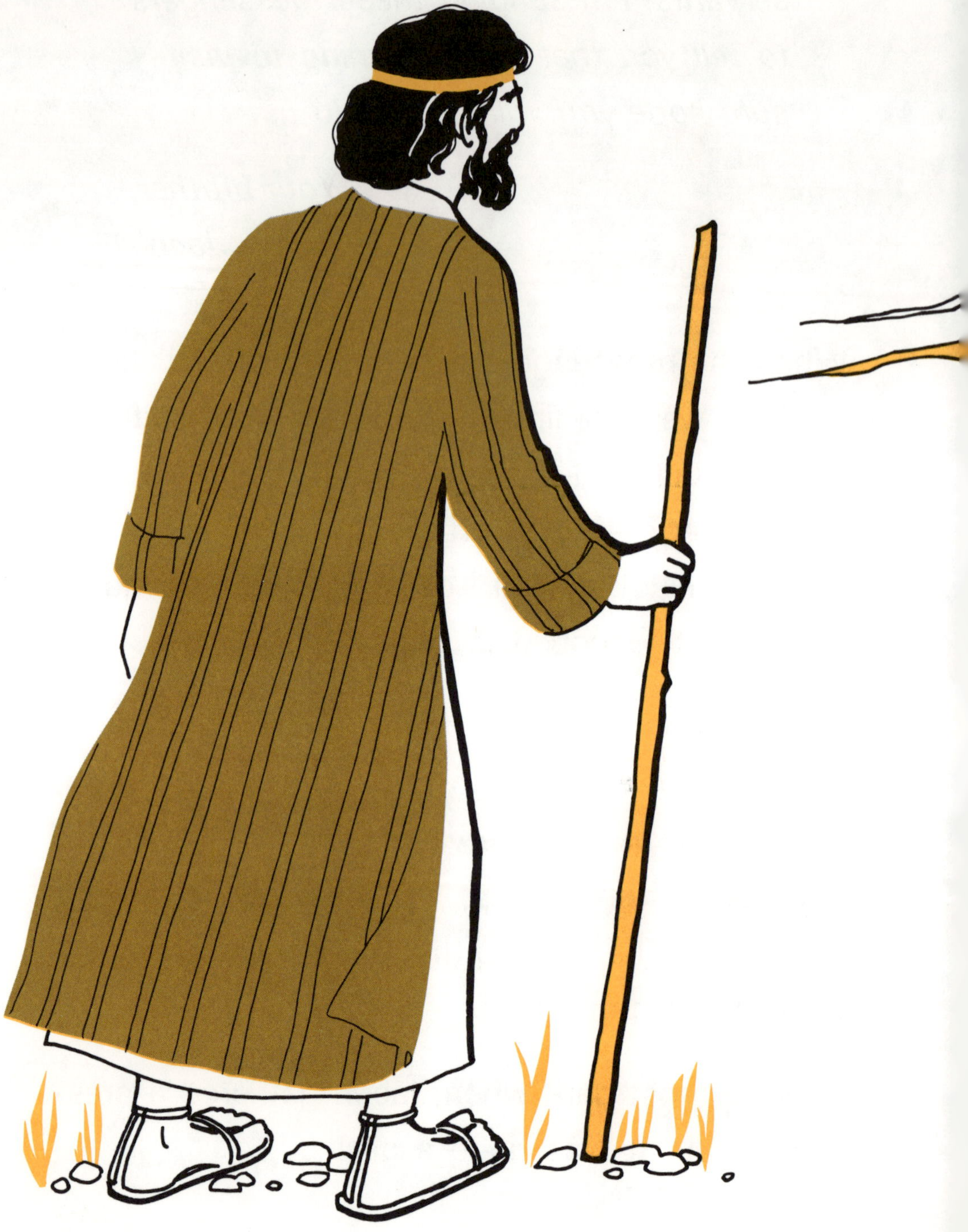

200 nanny goats
20 billy goats
220 sheep
30 camels and their colts
40 cows
10 bulls
30 donkeys

He sent messengers on ahead with these animals. He hoped, how he hoped, that Esau would get over being angry by the time he was given each of these herds.

Jacob tried to sleep, but he was restless. During the night he moved the people who were traveling with him across the brook. But Jacob came back to the other side of the stream. He wanted to be alone. Jacob prayed and wrestled with an angel of God. The angel touched Jacob's hip so that he would limp as he walked.

When it was almost day, Jacob received a wonderful blessing from God. Then as the sun rose, Jacob started out, limping.

After traveling a little way he thought he saw Esau way off in the distance. Jacob went ahead of his family. With every step he could see Esau more clearly. Jacob's heart was pounding. His hands were a bit sweaty. As he came near to Esau, Jacob bowed low seven times. When he finished, he looked up. For just a split second he waited. He wondered. He hoped.

Suddenly he saw Esau running toward him. His

hands and arms were open wide. Then before Jacob knew it, Esau was in his arms. They kissed! They hugged! They cried until tears raced down their faces. At long last they were brothers again! Jacob's prayer was answered!

RAGS TO RICHES

PART ONE

Genesis 42

Joseph was frantically busy. His grain store was the busiest place in Egypt. There was a terrible famine in the land. It wasn't only in Egypt, but also in many of the nearby countries. Nothing had grown, even the weeds were scrawny. So Joseph was kept pretty busy running the biggest business in Egypt.

One day several men came together into the store. They walked to Joseph's desk and bowed low before him. He looked up from his paperwork. His body fell hard against the back of his chair. It was almost too much of a shock. Before his eyes were his brothers. He counted quickly. Reuben, Simeon, Levi, Judah . . . everyone was there except Benjamin.

Joseph didn't want his surprise to show so he sat up quickly. He had recognized them immediately. But they didn't remember him. It had been so long since they had sold him as a slave. How would they have known about the years he spent in rags in prison? They probably thought he was dead by now. So he pretended.

"Where are you from?" He spoke gruffly.

"From Canaan. We came to buy grain."

"That's not true. I think you are spies. You've really come to spy on our land."

"Oh, no! Not at all! We're brothers. We still have a younger brother at home. We are all honest men. Please, sir! We are not spies."

"How do I know that?" Joseph turned his back toward them. How he wanted to cry. How much he loved them! He was thrilled to hear that young Benjamin was alive and well.

"Can't you take our word for it?"

"No, indeed! I will believe you only if one of you goes to Canaan and gets this brother you say you have."

"Oh, we couldn't! Our dear old Father Jacob wouldn't allow it. He already has one son dead. His name was Joseph. Father would die if anything happened to Benjamin too."

Joseph kept his brothers in Egypt for a few days. Then he sold them grain. He ordered his helpers to put each man's money back in the sack, on top. Then he sent them back to Canaan. All, that is, except Simeon. Simeon was kept in Egypt to be certain they would come again with Benjamin.

Late that night, the brothers stopped to rest. One of them opened his sack to give some grain to the animals. He discovered his money in the sack. Immediately the brothers were filled with terror. Who was this ruler in Egypt?

Why,

    just why,

        was he treating them so strangely?

PART TWO

Genesis 43, 44:1-2

At last all the grain was gone. There seemed to be no other choice. The brothers would have to return to Egypt. It was that or starve to death.

As much as Father Jacob disliked it, he knew he must let Benjamin go too. The ruler had said not to come back if they didn't bring their younger brother. Jacob told his sons to take honey, spices, nuts, and perfume. And he made sure they had enough money to buy more grain and pay again for the first grain. He wanted to be extra nice to this gruff young ruler of Egypt.

The brothers arrived safely in Egypt. They went straight to the palace. They tried to pay for the grain. But the doorman wouldn't accept the money. Instead he invited them in. He gave them fresh water to wash their feet. Their donkeys were fed. And they were asked to stay for lunch.

Things were becoming more and more confusing. Why was this man so gruff at one time and so nice at another? It was such a puzzle to them.

When Joseph arrived at noon, the brothers gave him their gifts. But Joseph was more interested in Benjamin. There in Joseph's own palace was his precious little brother. Joseph hurried from the room, tears pouring from his eyes.

Lying on his bed, he cried. He had so much love for Benjamin, for all of them. He couldn't keep it inside. It burst out in sobs. Joseph lay there until he felt better. Then he washed his face and returned to the room for lunch.

The brothers had a feast. Each of them ate until he was stuffed. Benjamin was especially full. He had been served five times more than the rest. Such a great time they had. It was like a party. Yet they still wondered about this unusual ruler.

Early the next morning, they left with grain. Again

Joseph told his helpers to put the money in the sacks. His own silver cup was to be put in Benjamin's sack. It was all part of Joseph's plan.

PART THREE

Genesis 44:3 — 45:1-9

The brothers were hardly out of the city when a messenger came galloping toward them. He came so fast that he left clouds of dust behind him. He stopped quickly in front of them.

"Why have you been so wicked? Why did you steal my master's silver cup?"

"Silver cup? What in the world are you talking about?"

"One of you must have it. The cup is gone!"

"Okay. Go ahead and search. If you find it in anyone's sack, you may kill him. And the rest of us will be your slaves."

"Fair enough! We won't kill him though. We will

keep him as a slave. The rest of you may go on home."

The search began. Sure enough! The cup was in Benjamin's sack. The brothers ripped their clothing. This just couldn't be! How could they ever explain this? It seemed impossible!

They arrived back at the palace. Judah explained everything to Joseph . . . everything about Father Jacob, Benjamin, and their dead brother, Joseph.

Joseph sent all of his servants out of the room. And then he burst into tears. He couldn't help but cry for joy. He sobbed so loudly that everyone in the palace could hear him.

He turned to his brothers.

"I am Joseph. Is m-my

father s-still alive?"

His body shook.

The brothers were stunned. They were so sure that Joseph was dead, long ago. They had torn off his coat and left him in rags in a pit. Then they

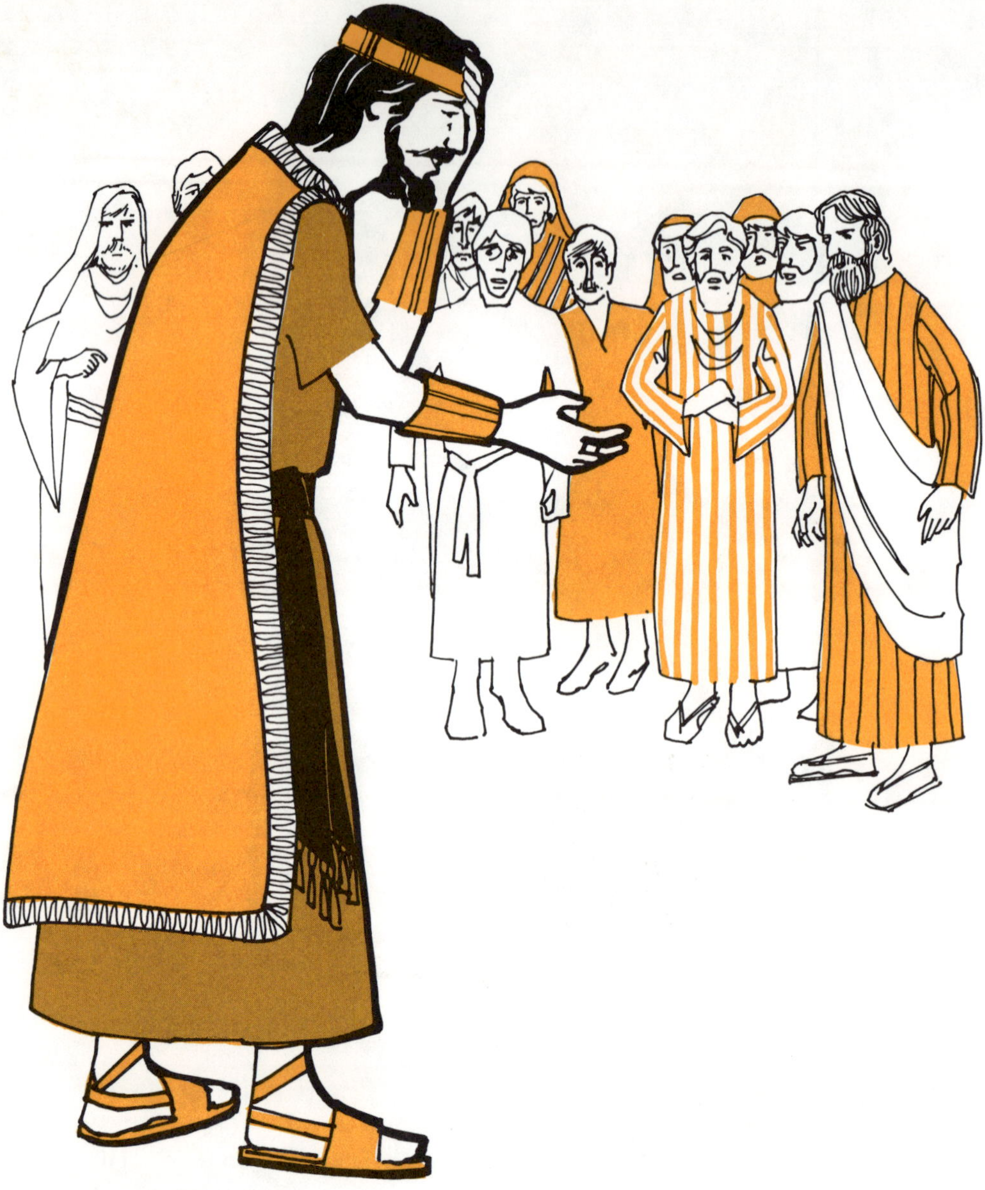

sold him as a slave. What was this man saying? They just stood there, silent and numb.

"C-come closer to me. I am Joseph, the same brother you sold. But don't worry about that now. God took care of me. I lived in prison in rags for a while. But now I am the ruler of Egypt. Go home and get my father. Tell him that Joseph is alive. Go quickly. I can hardly wait to see him again. Won't it be glorious for us to live together again as a family!"

Joseph thanked the Lord for this reunion. What a grand time they would have once more. And to think that God had planned it all!

A RHYTHM STORY — rhythm stories are explained on page 10.

THE CITY THAT CRASHED

Joshua 6:1-16

God	sent	spies	to	Jer-	i-	cho	
To	check	that	cit-	y's	might.		
God	had a	plan	to	smash	its	walls	
With-	out	a	blood-	y	fight.		
Josh-	ua	called	the	folks	to	come	
To	hear	a-	bout	God's	plan.		
Then	they	left	for	Jer-	i-	cho	
With	ev-	ery	lady	and	man.		
They	marched	a-	round	the	town	one	time
And	no	one	said	a	word.		
A	few	men	blew	their	trum-	pets,	
That's	all	that	could	be	heard.		

The guards upon the city wall
Watched them march that day.
"I wonder who they think they are?
It's silliness, I'd say!"

God's people kept on marching,
They kept it up six days;
But on the next they didn't stop.
The guards were sure amazed!

Seven times they marched around,
Then gave a mighty shout
That shook the heavy duty walls
'Til the bricks came popping out!

The noises of this great surprise
Were heard for miles around.
Those thick and sturdy city walls
Came crashing tumbling down!

Yes! God just tore them down!

THE MIGHTIEST MAN

PART ONE

Judges 16:4-21

Samson's strength was a real mystery. His enemies stared at his bulging, bouncing muscles. They oohed and aahed behind his back. He was certainly the strongest man anyone had ever known or heard about.

Now and then Samson did something spectacular . . . like tearing a roaring lion apart with his bare hands. Another time he caught three hundred wiggling, squiggling, clawing foxes and tied their tails together. Once he pulled the thick and heavy gates of a city right out of the ground. Then he carried them to the top of a mountain which was miles away. It was no wonder that his enemies were afraid of him. Yes, indeed, the Philistines were desperate. They were determined to discover the reason for Samson's mighty muscles.

The Philistines wanted to kill Samson as soon as they could. When they heard that Samson loved a Philistine woman named Delilah, they went to her house and demanded that she help them catch Samson. They offered her five thousand dollars if she would help. Delilah was wicked. She pretended to love Samson but she really loved the money she was going to get. Delilah began planning to learn the reason why Samson was so strong.

That very night she started. Sitting close to Samson, she begged. "Please, tell me why you're so strong. I'd like to know, Samson."

"Well, Delilah, it's this way. If someone tied me with seven raw-leather strings, I'd be as weak as any other man."

Delilah had the seven strings brought to her immediately. While Samson was sleeping she tied them tightly around his wrists and ankles.

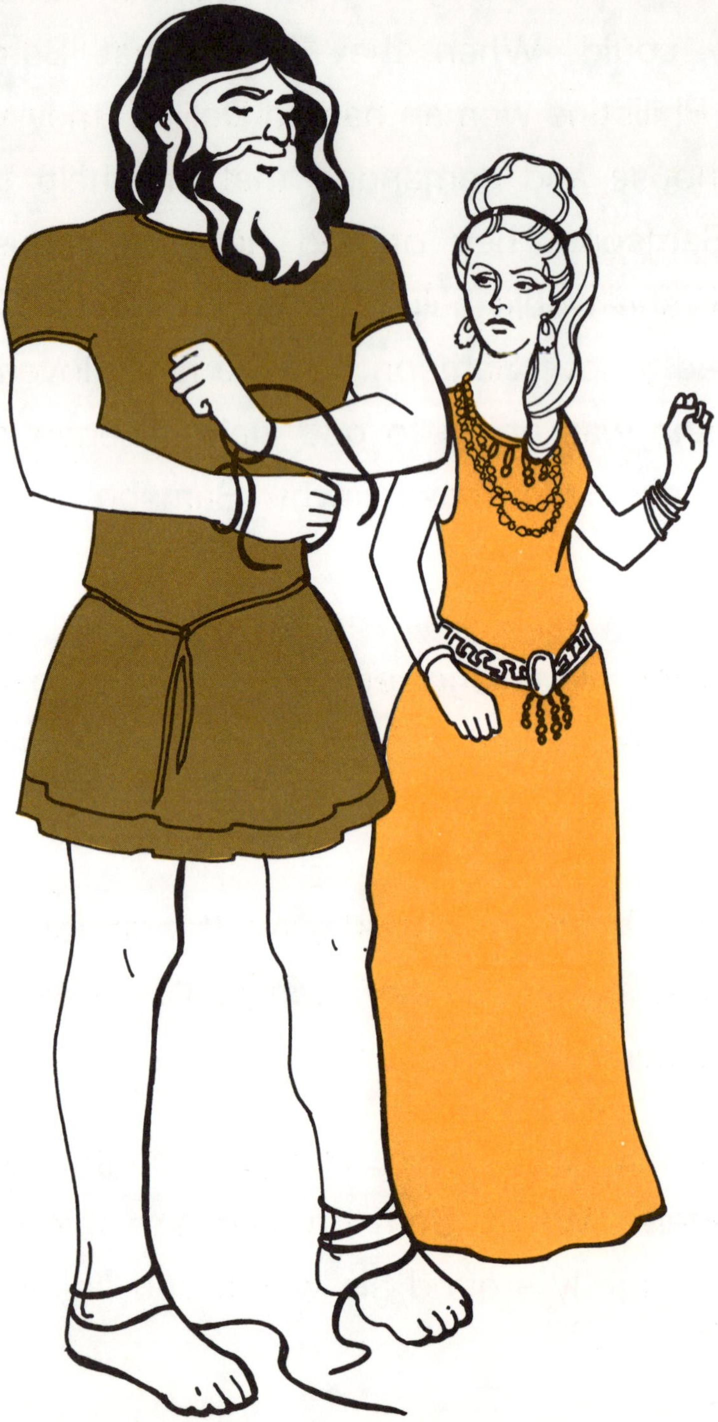

Then she called, "Samson! Quick! The Philistines are here!"

Samson jumped up. The leather strings snapped off in a split second.

Delilah was angry. "Now, Samson, that wasn't nice! You're teasing me. Stop lying and tell me the truth. How can anyone capture you? Is it possible?"

"Okay, Delilah. If you tied me with new rope, I'd be pretty weak. But remember, the ropes have to be brand new, not used at all!"

As Samson slept that night, Delilah did just that. She tied him with knots of the newest, stiffest, strongest rope she could find. Meanwhile the Philistine men were hiding in the next room, waiting.

When she had everything ready, she cried excitedly. "Samson, the Philistines are here to capture you!"

He jumped quickly. The ropes fell off like soggy spiderwebs. Samson still had not told the truth.

Again she begged, more and more angrily. She complained and demanded. So Samson told her that if his long hair were woven right in with the cloth she was weaving, he'd be as weak as a flea.

But Delilah was tricked again. When she called him, he jerked so quickly that he broke her cloth-making frame into little twig-size pieces. The pieces were scattered in heaps on the floor.

"Samson, honey, how can you say you love me when you lie to me like this? It's just a big joke to you. Won't you please tell me the truth? Please?"

Finally Samson could stand it no longer. She had nagged and whined for so many days. So he explained it to her.

"All right, Delilah. You see, my hair has never been cut. I am God's servant and I may not cut my hair. If I did, I would be breaking God's command. Then I would truly be weak. God would take away every ounce of my strength."

Delilah was thrilled. This time she knew she had the truth. She called the Philistine leaders to come to her house. She asked them to bring the money with them. Tonight would be the night at last!

While Samson slept, a barber snipped his hair and shaved his head. When the barber was finished, Samson's head was smooth and bald. God's command had been disobeyed.

Proudly Delilah called. "Samson, the Philistines are here to capture you!"

Samson jumped up. He saw the men coming toward him with ropes and chains. He raised his arms and hands to grab them. As he did, his muscles felt limp—saggy and baggy. His arms felt like jelly. His bones were like rubber. The once strong and mighty Samson was tied quickly and easily.

PART TWO

Judges 16:22-30

Samson moved his arms 'round and 'round and 'round. He ground grain at the prison mill. He was chained to the floor. There was no chance of escape. He couldn't see at all because his captors had taken his eyes. Blind, weak Samson made flour day after day after day.

One day while Samson was grinding grain, the Philistines had a party to celebrate the capture of Samson. As they ate and drank, they became silly from too much wine. Just for fun they demanded that Samson be brought out so they could tease him.

As Samson was led out of the prison, the people giggled. Some rolled over from laughing. To be sure that everyone could see weak and flabby Samson, he was put in the center of the room. He stood right between two tall pillars that held up the roof.

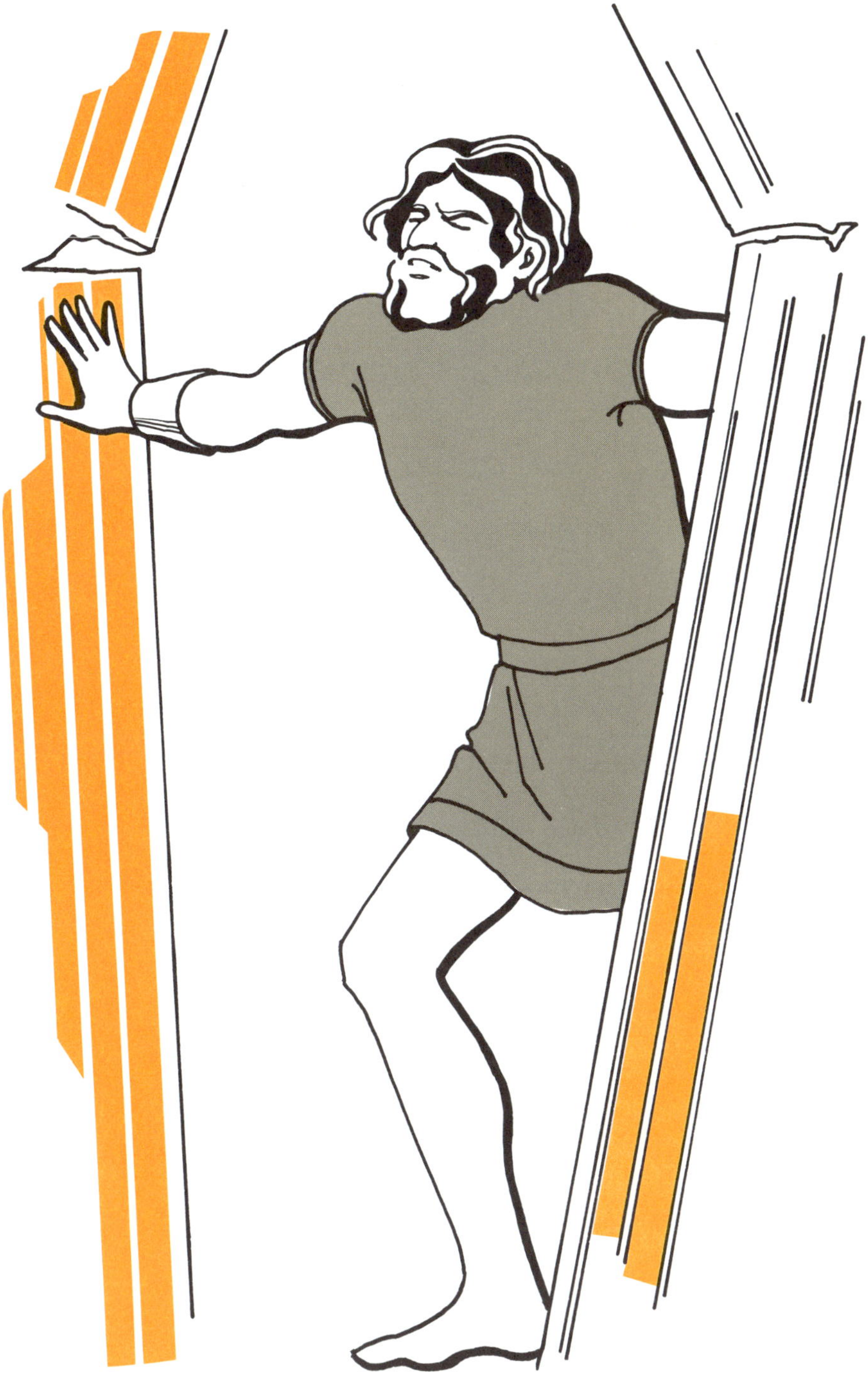

Samson couldn't see, but he could hear their teasing. They sounded like they thought they were so smart.

Samson leaned over to talk to the boy who had led him from the prison. "Put my hands on the pillars. I want to rest against them."

The boy did just that. Then Samson prayed. "Oh Lord! Remember me again. Give me strength one more time. Then I can pay these Philistines for taking at least one of my eyes."

He stopped. He pushed against the pillars. Every muscle of his body tightened and pushed. Then he continued his prayer. "Let me die with the Philistines."

The temple cracked, then crashed madly. Bricks, doors, and dirt flew helter-skelter. The people in the balconies were thrown through the air. Three thousand Philistines were killed. And Samson's life was over.

WHIRLWIND TO HEAVEN

II Kings 2:7-14

There was so much excitement. Elijah was going to heaven! His helper, Elisha, knew it too. So did all the students at the seminary. The news spread so quickly because this had never happened before. Imagine it! The Lord let Elijah know the exact day he would be taken to heaven. It was so well planned. He knew just the spot where he was to wait.

The place chosen was near the Jordan River. Elijah and Elisha walked together. As they came to the river, Elijah suggested that Elisha stay behind. Elijah wanted to be alone for his trip to heaven. But Elisha wouldn't let Elijah out of his sight. So they walked along together. Some of the seminary students stayed behind, watching.

They came to the river. It was deep, much too deep to wade across. Elijah took off his coat. He folded it carefully together. Using it as a whip, he struck the water. Smack! Splash! The water separated. All the way across, from one bank to the other, the water divided. The miracle of it was that the bottom was not mucky and muddy. It was absolutely dry! Elijah and Elisha crossed the river on their own private path! When they were on the other side, the water splashed back together again.

Elijah was anxious. He had so little time left. But there was one more thing he wanted to ask Elisha. "Before I go, is there anything you want from me?"

"Yes, please.

Treat me as your firstborn son.

Give me a double portion

of your spirit."

"Well, Elisha. You asked for a pretty tough thing. If you see me go to heaven, the answer is yes. If you don't, then the answer is no."

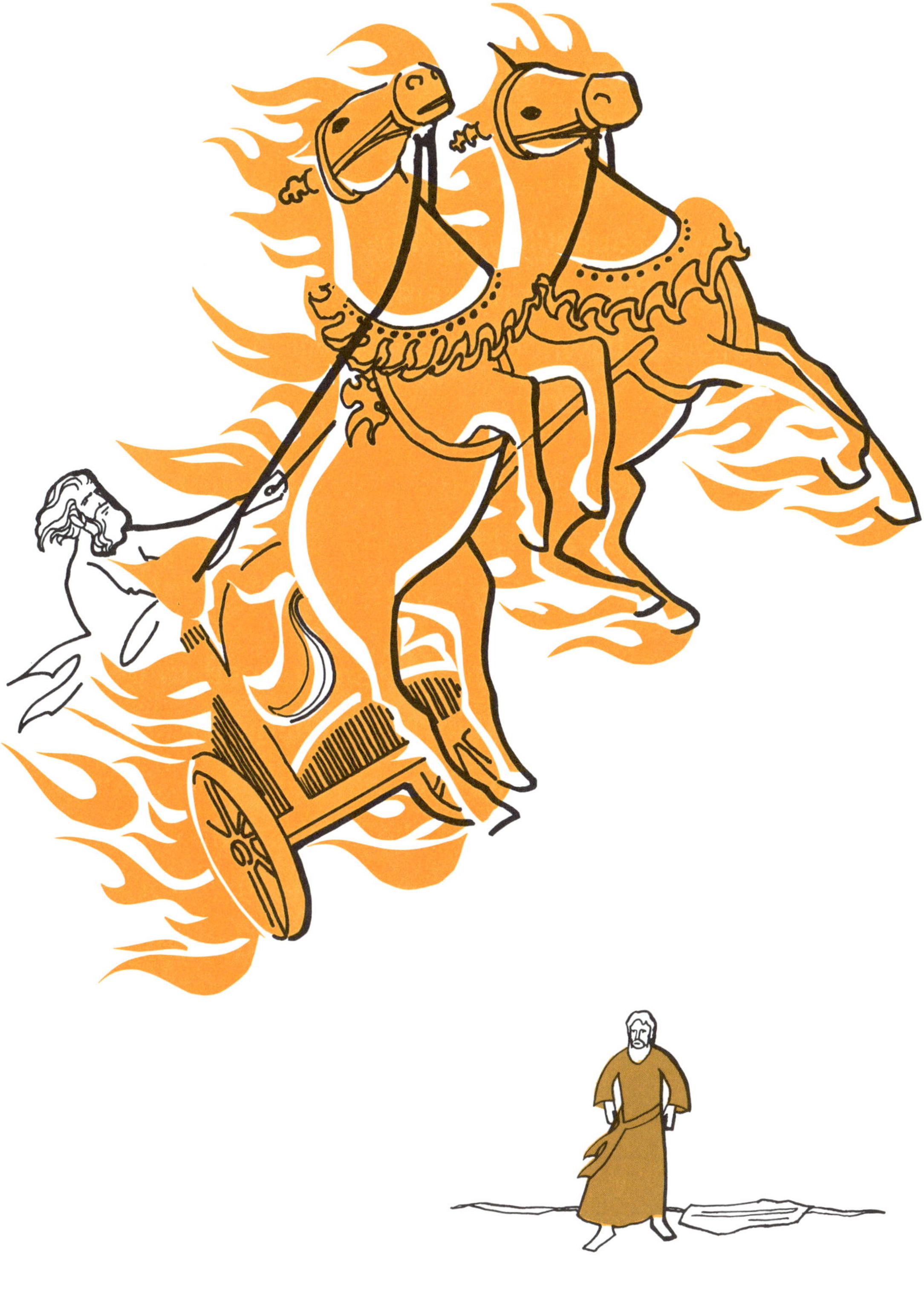

Their talking ended right there. From nowhere a chariot of fire appeared. It came straight toward them. Fiery horses were pulling it. They galloped. They were speeding right between Elijah and Elisha. Just as the chariot came between, there was a whirlwind. It whooshed and swirled and took Elijah straight to heaven.

Elisha cried out. "My father! My father!" As he did, the chariot disappeared. Elijah was gone. His coat lay in a heap on the ground.

Stooping to pick it up, Elisha turned to go home. He walked slowly, thinking. When he came to the Jordan River he hit the water with Elijah's coat, just as Elijah had done. Again the water separated. He walked across, just as before. Only this time he was alone. He wouldn't, he couldn't ever forget this miracle. He'd seen it with his own eyes. He'd heard the wind. Elijah was in heaven! He was living with God, talking with God . . . loving God!

RESCUE BY ROPE
PART ONE

Jeremiah 38:1-13; 39:15-18

Jeremiah was God's prophet. He gave messages from God to the people in Jerusalem. Lately he'd been giving some strange messages. At least some people thought so. Jeremiah told the people that they should not fight the Babylonians anymore. He said that they should surrender. They should let the Babylonian king take over Jerusalem.

Naturally the princes were furious! They had been trying to convince the soldiers to keep fighting. Meanwhile Jeremiah was saying just the opposite. The princes forgot that Jeremiah was speaking God's message. The princes decided that it would be easy enough to get rid of Jeremiah and his silly messages. All they had to do was kill him. So off they went to see the king!

"King Zedekiah, thank you for seeing us today. We're here to speak with you about a dreadful problem with Jeremiah. We would like permission to kill him." They were so angry that they all tried to talk at once.

"Kill him?

Why?"

"He's telling everyone to sit back and surrender. Here we are trying to fight the Babylonians. Then he comes along and talks like that!" When one finished talking, they all nodded their heads in agreement.

"Well, all right. Do whatever you want. I guess I can't stop you." The king rose from his throne and left the room.

Since the princes had wanted to get rid of Jeremiah before, they had a plan ready. They took him to a water pit and lowered him into the hole. Then they shook hands together. Their little plan had worked. How sure they were that Jeremiah would starve to death in that stinking old hole.

Jeremiah had landed with a rolling thud. Fortunately it wasn't dry and hard at the bottom. There was just enough water to make soupy mud. The mud oozed over his feet and in between his toes.

He felt it sucking his feet down . . . down . . . down. He kept trying to climb out. But that was impossible. He had no choice but to sit down in it. The mud swallowed him up to his waist.

PART TWO

Ebed-melech heard that Jeremiah was in the pit. He was pretty sure he could do something about it. After all, he knew the king very well. In fact, Ebed-melech was an important man in the kingdom. He rushed out to the courtyard.

"My lord, the king, hear me! Those men that put Jeremiah in the pit have done a terrible thing. You know he will die in there. He'll starve to death!"

"Yes, I suppose he will."

"But please, King Zedekiah, we must do something about it. Please, may I help him? He's God's messenger. Let me pull him out!"

"All right, Ebed-melech. You may. Take some men and whatever you need. Get Jeremiah out quickly before he dies." King Zedekiah smiled kindly at Ebed-melech. He had always been such a good servant and so kind.

Ebed-melech called the men to meet at the palace. They went to the basement and got some rags and old clothes. On the way out, they got the ropes. They ran out the door to the water pit.

Ebed-melech got down on his knees. He lowered his head into the hole. "Jeremiah?"

"Yes? Who is it?"

"It's me, Ebed-melech. We're here to help you."

"Say, that's great. I prayed that the Lord might send someone to get me out of here."

"Well, we're here. I'm sending down a bundle of old clothes. Untie the rope and take them."

"What are they for?"

"Put them under your arms. Then when you put the rope around your body, it won't rub against your bare skin."

"Say, you really came prepared. Okay, I'm ready."

"Got the ropes in place?"

"Yep. Let's go!"

Ebed-melech gave the orders: "Ready, set, pull!"

Together they pulled, slowly and carefully. Each man had a good firm hold on his part of the rope. With those strong men helping, Jeremiah didn't seem very heavy. In less than two minutes, Jeremiah's head was at the top. While some of them held the rope, others ran to help Jeremiah out.

Jeremiah thanked God for the rescue. And he also thanked Ebed-melech. Later when the city was destroyed, God kept Ebed-melech safe. Ebed-melech was safe because he trusted God and His messenger.

A RHYTHM STORY — rhythm stories are explained on page 10.

A STRANGE PLACE TO SPEND THE NIGHT

Jonah 1 and 2

God	came	and	talked	to	Jo-	nah	
And	gave	him	this	com-	mand:		
"You	go	to	wick-	ed	Nin-	e-	vah
Be-	fore	I	wreck	that	land."		

But Jonah didn't want to go,
He thought that he could hide.
He got on board a waiting ship
And fell a-sleep in-side.

But God was watch-ing Jonah,
God made the o-cean roar.
Jonah knew it was his fault
He asked to be thrown over-board.

God sent a mon-strous hungry fish
That swal-lowed Jonah quickly;
When three days and nights had passed,
That fish was feel-ing sick-ly.

Quick as scat it swam to shore
And heaved a mighty URP!
It got rid of Jonah. God's work.
He was read-y for God's work.

It got rid of Jonah. God's
He was read-y for God's work.

186

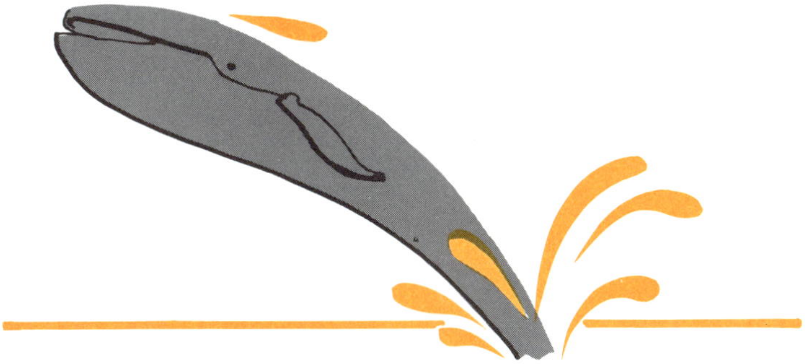

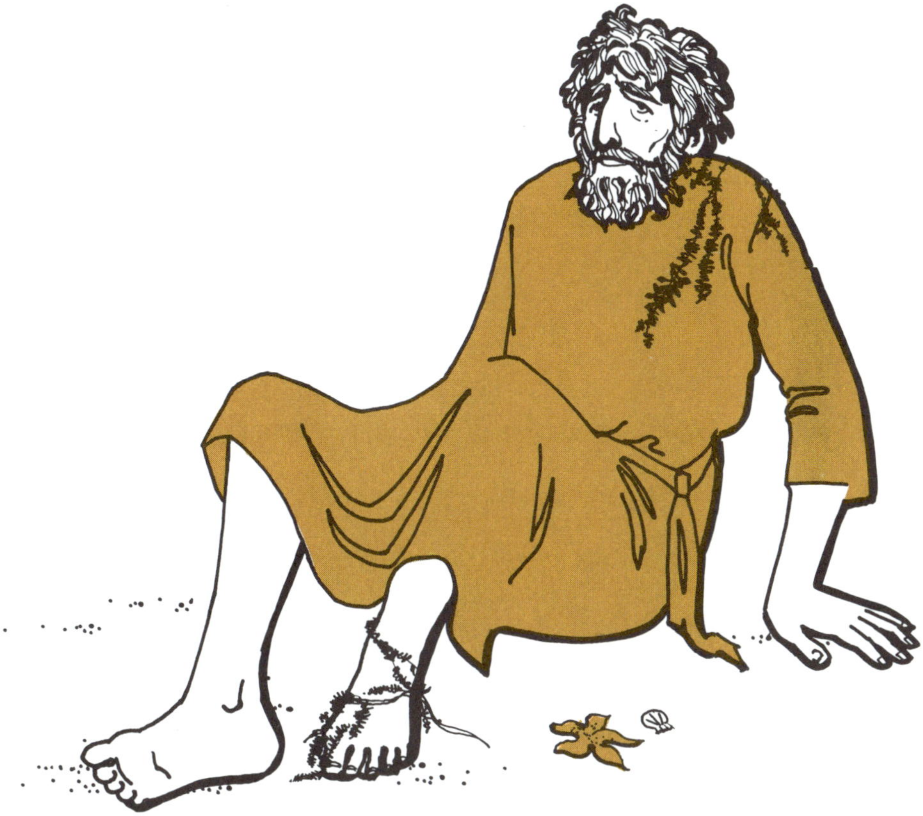

JOHN THE BAPTIZER

Matthew 3:1-6, 13-17

Every time I heard that voice I knew it was John's. His voice was clear. He spoke loudly. I could tell that he believed in what he was saying. Most any day, in the fields around Judea, I could find him calling.

"Turn away from your sin!

Repent!

You must look to God.

He is coming soon!"

We all called him John the Baptist. That's because he baptized people. Anyone who was sorry for his sins could be baptized, if he believed that God forgave his sins.

It was fun to hear John preach. I always liked to see his clothes. They were a little different. His coat was made out of camel's hair. He always wore the same brown leather belt around his waist. A few times I saw him eating supper. He ate honey that wild bees made. And he ate those jumping bugs. We call them locusts. Even his food was odd, you'd have to agree.

I just happened to be there the day all the excitement happened. I had finished my chores early. So mom let me go. I usually sat real close to the river bank whenever John was baptizing people. I liked to watch John get in the water. All the people followed him, wading slowly into the river, waiting for their turn to be baptized.

On this particular day, Jesus came. John was so surprised to see Him I remember exactly what happened, almost word for word.

"John, I'd like you to baptize me."

"Oh, no! I couldn't! I shouldn't! It wouldn't be right. You ought to baptize me!"

"Please do it, John. I have to do it the way God wants. And He wants you to baptize me."

"If you insist, Jesus, I will do it. Come in the water with me."

John waded into the river. He never went in too deep. It was about up to his waist. Jesus followed behind him. Everyone along the riverside waited curiously.

The baptism went just like any other. It was what happened afterward that made me know that Jesus was really the Son of God. A loud, loud voice thundered from heaven. It said,

"This is my beloved Son,

and I am wonderfully pleased

with Him."

Jesus looked up when He came out of the river. He saw a beautiful dove gliding from heaven. It was the Spirit of God.

That clinched it! I knew for sure that everything John the Baptist said was true! God's kingdom was really coming. It was here right now! I'd seen it all with my own eyes. I hurried home just as fast as my six-year-old legs could carry me. I couldn't wait to tell my folks!

THE GRAVEYARD MONSTER

Mark 5:1-13

Legion is my name. I live in the graveyard and run around the gravestones. I admit it's a strange place to stay. But it's the only place I may stay. The town people call me crazy. You should see them scatter away whenever they see me. No one wants me to come anywhere near him.

Sometimes people try to put handcuffs on me so I'm not so wild. But I just laugh and shriek in their faces. Chain me? Impossible! I'm so strong that I smash their silly chains. I can snap off chains of iron as easily as if they were made of string. No one can hold me. No one and nothing could ever keep me quiet.

You see, I'm not really crazy. I'm just full of evil spirits and ideas. They make me scream, kick, jump, and holler. I roll on the ground, giggle, and cry. I can't help it. I can't sit still. I can't think

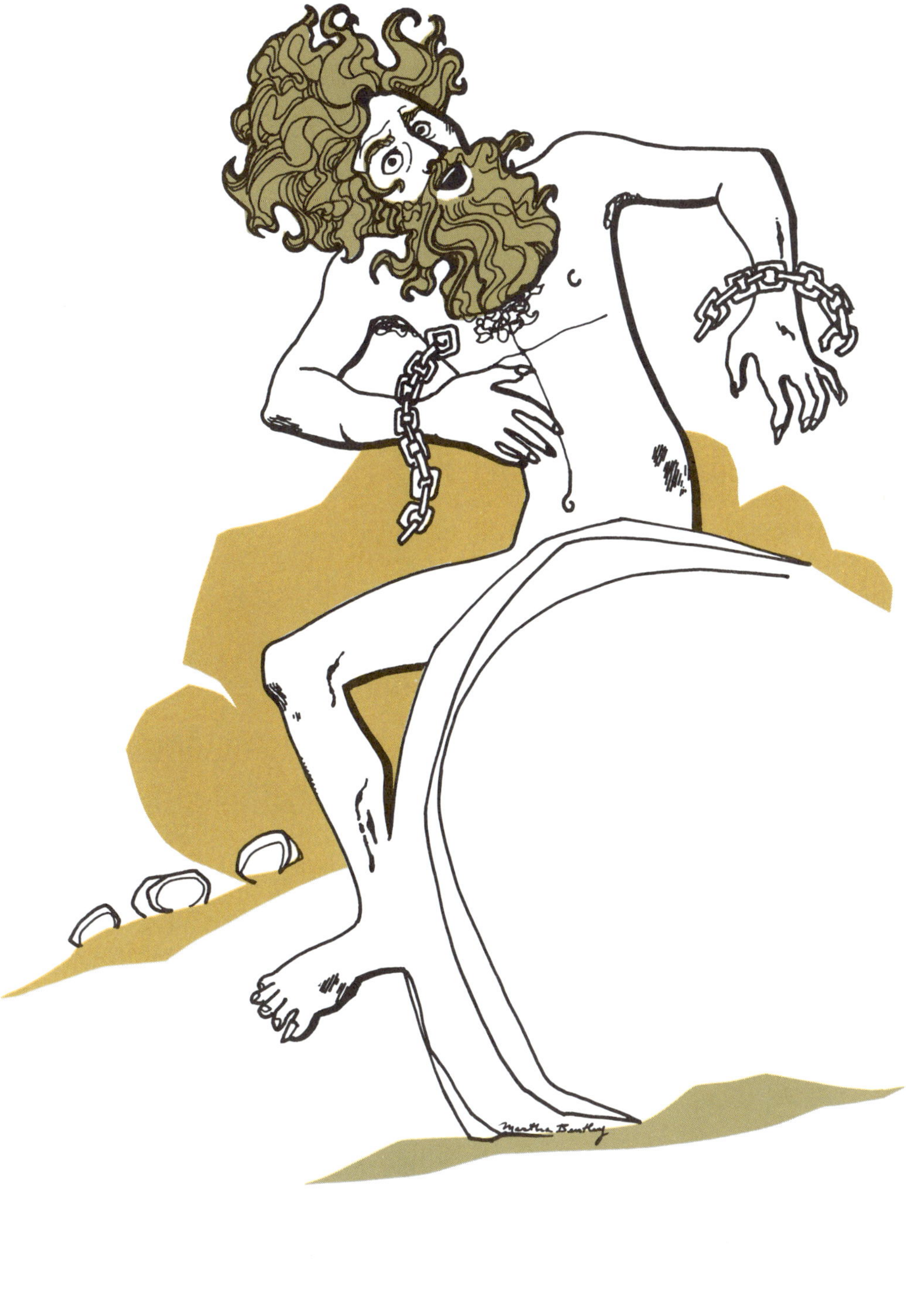
Martha Bentley

straight. I can't do anything at all but act like a wild man.

It's no wonder the folks around here are afraid of me. I don't wear any clothes. I'm filthy. My hair is stuck together like that of a dirty animal's. I roll in the mud. I smell like garbage. I'm such a mess. I look just like a monster.

What scares them the most, though, is the way I act. Sometimes I'm so wild I cut myself on sharp stones. I can't help it. I guess I act like a monster too.

One day, while I was rolling and screaming behind the gravestones, I saw a boat coming toward shore. A man was climbing out. I'm not sure why, but I ran just as fast as I could. I ran straight for him. I fell on my knees. I laid in front of Him, panting like a dog. The man was Jesus.

He looked down at me and spoke. "Come out, you evil spirits!"

I screamed and cried. "What are you trying to do to me, Jesus? Don't torture me this way."

"What is your name?" He asked so calmly and politely. He wasn't afraid of me.

"Legion. There are a lot of evil spirits in me. But please don't send them away." I could hear myself talking. I wondered what Jesus would do with me.

"Come out of this man, you devils! Go to the pigs over on the hill." He stood quietly and waited.

I felt strange, stranger than I've ever felt before. My head was clearing up. I could think straight. Then my arms fell to my side, resting. Then my body didn't shake so funny. My legs were relaxed and free. For the very first time in my life I could be quiet and still.

And the devils? I wondered where they went. Jesus had told them to bother the pigs. I looked up just in time to see those pigs. Every one of them began snorting and squealing. They kicked their legs and pushed with their snouts. They pell-melled so fast that they galloped right down the hillside and into the lake. Each of them drowned.

For the first time I really saw myself. I could smell the garbage odor. I rushed off to take a bath and clean up a bit. I put on clothes and combed my hair. Then I hurried back to Jesus.

How surprised the people were! It scared them that I was . . . clean. I was sitting still on the grass. I had clothes on, nice clothes. I could talk straight. Thank God He made me a real person again!

THE BOLD FISHERMAN

Jesus had twelve disciples. These were special men that Jesus called to help Him. One of them was named Peter. His name means "rock."

That may sound like a strange name to you. It was a good name for Peter. He was strong and bold and loud. He liked to brag. Usually he was the first one of the twelve disciples to speak up. Often the others let him be the speaker for the whole group. He was always the talker and the leader.

In spite of Peter's bragging, you will learn to love him just as Jesus did. These four short stories and the song will tell you a little more about Peter, the fisherman.

PART ONE

Luke 5:1-11

My name is Peter. Early one morning I had quite an experience. I was busy cleaning my fish nets. I had just rinsed them carefully when Jesus came wading to my boat. So many people were around Him, pushing and shoving to get near Him.

First thing I knew, He had jumped in. There He stood, looking at me. He asked me to row out a little way from shore. That would make it easier for Him to talk to the people without being crushed by them.

That was all right with me. He didn't talk such a long time anyway. When He was finished, He told me to go out to deeper water. He even promised I'd get a big catch!

Big catch? Ha! That was a joke. We'd worked hard. All night long we'd been fishing. We didn't catch a thing! Not even a minnow. I didn't want to sound rude. Besides, He insisted. So I went out into deeper water.

My friend and I unfolded our clean nets. We weren't working too well at this late hour of the morning. We were tired from fishing all night. But we threw the nets in the water anyway.

Just as soon as I let those nets over the edge, they disappeared. It felt like a whale had hold of them! It took me just a minute to open my drooping eyes wide enough to see what was weighing down the nets, it was . . .

    fish,
       fish,
          fish,
             and more fish!

I didn't have time to blink more than once. There were so many slippery, slimy fish I couldn't haul them in fast enough. While I called for help I heard a loud r-r-rip! Then another and another. Imagine that! My nets were empty all night. And now there were so many fish that they were wrecking the nets!

I filled my boat as fast as I could. We filled my friend's boat too. In fact, we filled them so full, we nearly sank our boats!

Then all of a sudden the idea hit me. This man wasn't just any regular man. This man was Jesus. I fell right on my knees. "Oh, sir, please leave us fishermen alone. I'm too much of a sinner to be around You!"

I'll just never forget His answer. He said, "Don't let that worry you. From now on you're going to help Me find men. You'll be a fisher of men instead of a fisher of fish!"

Just as soon as we got back to shore, we went with Jesus. I knew that someone would take the fish to market and mend the nets. I didn't have time for it. I had to be with Jesus!

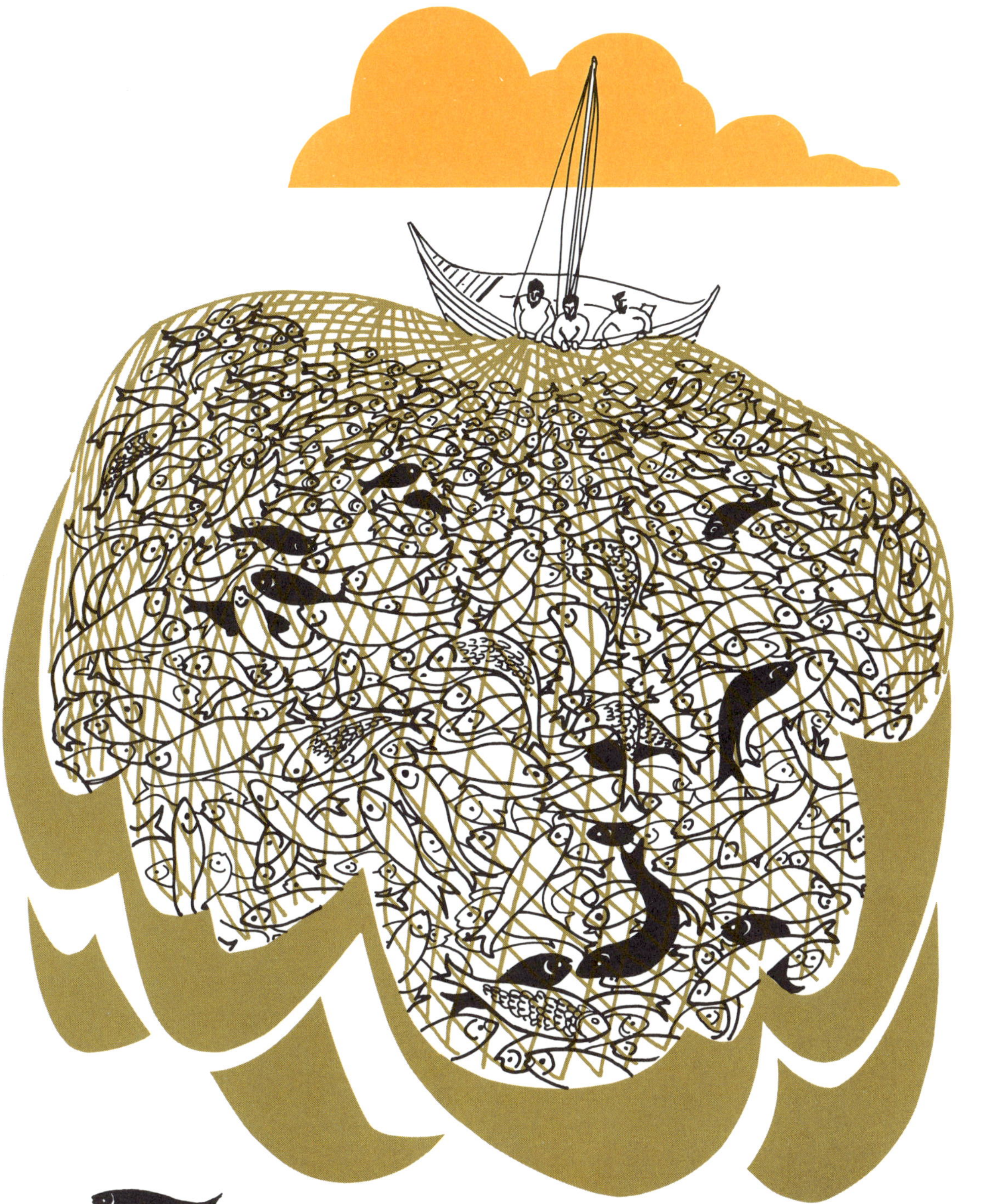

PART TWO

I WILL MAKE YOU FISHERS OF MEN

Harry D. Clarke

1. "I will make you fish-ers of men, fish-ers of men, fish-ers of men; I will make you fish-ers of men if you come un-to me;"
2. Hear Christ call-ing, "Come un-to me, come un-to me, come un-to me;" Hear Christ call-ing, "Come un-to me, I will

fol - low me. If you fol - low me, if you fol - low me;
give you rest. I will give you rest, I will give you rest;"

I will make you fish-ers of men if you fol - low me."
Hear Christ call-ing,"Come un - to me, I will give you rest."

Copyright, 1927. Renewal, 1955 by H. Clarke. Assigned to Hope Publishing Company. All rights reserved. Used by permission.

PART THREE

Matthew 14:22-33

The crowds had been pretty heavy lately. After one tiring day Jesus told the twelve of us to get in the boat and cross the lake. He wanted to stay and help the people start for home. Then He went alone to pray.

Meanwhile we were in real trouble. It was after midnight. Winds were sweeping across the lake. Waves tossed our little boat around like a paper cup. Each of us worried about drowning.

Right in the middle of all this we had a second scare. Out in the distance we saw what looked like a ghost coming toward us. It was actually walking on the water. You can believe that we screamed until our throats were sore!

"Don't be afraid!" came the voice. When we heard that, we were pretty sure it was Jesus. It sounded like Him.

Just to be doubly sure, I called. "If it's really You, tell me that I can walk on the water to meet You."

"All right, Peter. Come along!"

When I heard Him call me by name, I climbed right out. I actually got out of the boat and walked on those steep and slippery waves. As long as I thought about the Jesus I loved and trusted, I was all right.

Once I glanced down and saw the water, the deep and angry water. That scared me. I forgot all about Jesus right then. All I could think about was me, drowning me!

"Save me! Lord! Save me!" I panicked! Surely Jesus could see that I was about to be swallowed alive by the furious waves!

Instantly Jesus' hand reached out. He looked down at me and pulled me up. "Oh, Peter! You have so little faith. Why didn't you trust me?"

I felt ashamed. Jesus was right. I started out so quickly, so proud, so sure I could do it. Then I doubted. I forgot about my powerful Lord.

The others watched us as we climbed into the boat. After we were in the boat the waves tiptoed off and the wind drifted far away. It was all such a tremendous miracle. All of us shook our heads. It was almost unbelievable, but true, so true! We cried out, "Jesus! You really are the Son of God! You really are!"

PART FOUR

John 18:1-11

We were expecting trouble. The word was going around that Jesus might be captured. I took my sword along just in case. One just never knows when one might need it.

We were in the orchard. Jesus had been praying. Wouldn't you know it! I fell asleep. So did

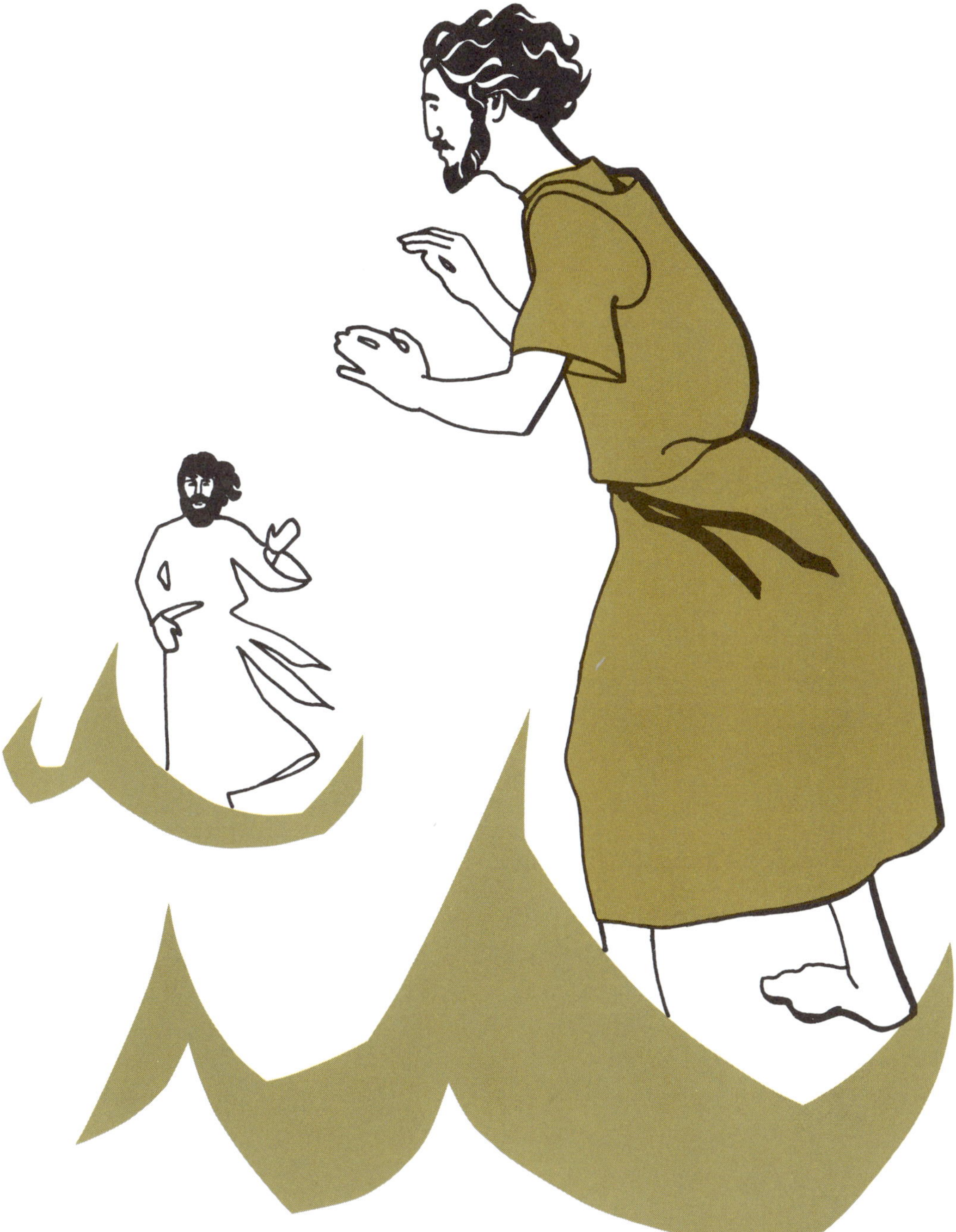

a few of the others. Almost before we woke up, the soldiers were there.

Jesus asked who they wanted. They said they were looking for Jesus. When Jesus said that He was the man they wanted, they were so shocked they fell over. They couldn't believe that He was so honest. He didn't even try to run away!

While they were scrambling to get up, I saw my chance. If I was going to fight for my precious Jesus, I knew I'd better get busy! Quickly I swung my sword at one of the men. I hit him too . . . cut off his ear!

Jesus looked over at me. "Put your sword away, Peter. This isn't the time for fighting. I am supposed to go with these men."

We all watched while Jesus picked up the ear and put it back on the man's head. You'd think that the soldiers would have believed in Him. They stood right there and watched him perform a miracle. With just a touch, He healed a man's ear. But they didn't believe that Jesus was the Son of God. They took Jesus away. There I stood, alone with my sword.

I loved Jesus so much. I was only trying to help. Sometimes I just didn't understand. I guess that's what makes Him so wonderful. Precious Jesus loved me anyway. He loved me anyway!

PART FIVE

Acts 2:1-42

Exactly ten days after Jesus went to heaven, Peter and the small group of believers were together. They were celebrating one of the Jewish feasts. Eating, singing, praying, and praising, they continued their celebration. Oh, how they loved to be together.

The past ten days they had spent a lot of time together singing and praying. They were waiting for Jesus to send His Spirit. They waited in Jerusalem because Jesus had told them not even to leave town until He sent them this gift.

Right in the middle of their celebration, they heard an eerie, windy sound off in the distance. It was strange, like a siren howling. They could easily hear the howling above their singing. The windy sound became louder and stronger, and seemed to be coming closer. Swirling, rolling, and blowing it came until it settled above the very house where they were meeting.

Thaddeus and Thomas ran to the windows to look out. Bartholomew, Philip, and Simon began opening doors and windows. Matthias called: "There's nothing blowing around in the street. Yet I hear the wind. What is going on? What can it be?"

On and on the windy sound continued, powerful and frightening. The roaring filled the house and spilled outside. Confused, the believers looked around. Covering their ears, they tried to block out the ringing noise.

Peter hollered out above the noise. "John, Matthew, James. All of you! Do you see it too? Above each of your heads is a flickering flame of fire!" Peter's eyes were wide and wondering.

Just as he said that, he knew. Peter knew for sure. So did the others. The very thing, the gift they were waiting for was here! The Holy Spirit had come! Together they praised God! Yes, they were praising God. Each one praised God in a different language! It was most unusual!

By this time the city people were running and pushing their way toward the house. Soon there was quite a crowd outside the house. People were shoving and squeezing each other trying to find out about this weird noise.

Peter and the other believers came out to speak to the people. The believers spoke in new languages, languages they had never learned before. Yes, some of the languages they had never even heard before! Yet they spoke these strange words clearly, loudly, and perfectly. Many people heard the story of Jesus in their own language for the first time. The Holy Spirit had given the believers this power.

"What is going on?" called a visitor, running to Peter.

"Aw, it's nothing!" answered a man from across the street. "It's just a bunch of drunks."

Peter stood up so that the crowd could see him. The other disciples gathered around him. Peter, yes, lovable and quick-speaking Peter had something to say, something to shout!

"Drunk? These men haven't had even a drop of wine. What you have seen and heard is God's Holy Spirit coming upon us, just as He promised. God's Spirit gives us power to speak boldly and clearly about our Lord."

"Listen, people! You can have this same gift. You must turn away from sinning and be baptized. Then the Holy Spirit will be yours. God has promised it to everyone who believes."

Peter continued preaching. He told more and more about Jesus. It was a very long sermon. On that day alone, Peter's sermon was heard by thousands of people. Three thousand believed in Jesus right there and were baptized.

Praise! Praise the Lord!

A RHYTHM STORY — rhythm stories are explained on page 10.

THE PLAN THAT HEALED A FRIEND

Luke 5:18-26

There	once	was a	man
Who	couldn't	walk a	bit,
But at	least	he could	talk
Tho' his	arms and	legs were	stiff.
His	friends	heard the	news
That the	Lord was	coming	soon;
So they	put him	on a	cot
And	sang a	happy	tune.

They	took him	to the	house
But	saw that	it was	packed.
Now	what a-	bout their	plan?
Would they	have to	take him	back?
They	climbed	to the	roof
'Cause	it was	nice and	flat.
They	made a	great big	hole
And	let him	down through	that.
The	Lord	said, "My	son,
I've	washed your	sins a-	way.
And be-	cause	you be-	lieve,
You can	walk to-	day.	
And be-	cause	you be-	lieve,
You can	throw that	bed a-	way!

215

TEN LEPERS

Bright ($\quarter = 144$)

Ten unclean and nowhere to go.
Ten men cleansed as clean as snow. One returned to give God thanks, but nine went away.

1. Ten men, lepers in a Hebrew town. Ten crying:
2. "Lord, make me clean," was their single cry. "See, how the

©MCMLXV by Medical Mission Sisters, Philadelphia, Pa.
Sole selling agent Vanguard Music Corp., 250 West 57th St., New York, N.Y. 10019.
All rights reserved. Permission granted to reprint by Vanguard Music Corp.

"Ten Lepers" is available on album AVS 101 from Avant Garde Records Inc., 250 W. 57th Street, N.Y., N.Y. 10019

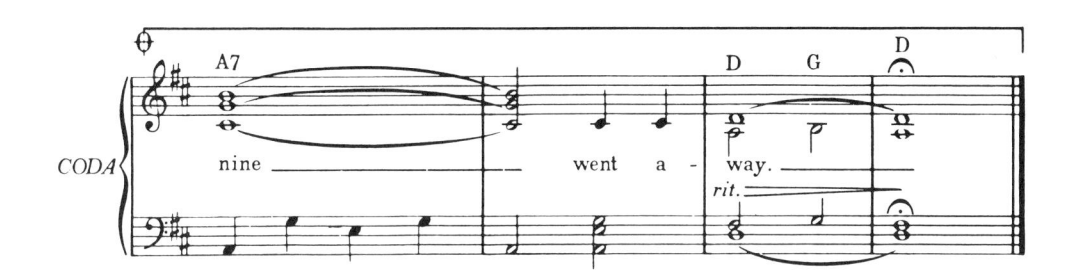

3. Like a tree when its buds come true,
   or a patch of spring that is fresh and new,
   Christ restored the ones defiled,
   gave them the flesh of a new-born child.

4. God gives gifts to us ev'ry day,
   favors His people in ev'ry way;
   Hope restored and pain relieved--
   Do you ever give thanks for a gift received?

5. Thank you, Lord, for the summer sun,
   for sight and song and good deeds done,
   faith and family and loving friends,
   for the day that begins and the night that ends.

A RHYTHM STORY — rhythm stories are explained on page 10.

JUST ONE CAME BACK

Luke 17:11-19

Their	skin	was	sore	and	rot-	ten,
These	ten	poor	help-	less	men;	
Man-	y	days	they	won-	dered,	
Can	we	be	well	a-	gain?	

Then	one	day	Je-	sus	saw	them,
They	cried	out	loud	to	Him,	
"Je-	sus,	Mas-	ter,	help	us!	
Please	make	us	well	a-	gain!"	

Jesus answered kindly,
"Go straight to see the priest;
Show him that your skin is clean,
That you've been healed indeed!"

They hurried toward the temple;
But wait! Can this be real?
Their skin was fresh and new again—
They knew they had been healed!

Yet only one came running back
To thank the Lord that day.
Jesus saw this man's great faith,
And washed his sins away!

ZACCHEUS

Calypso (♩=88)

(Maracas)

(Wood Block)

was a man in Jer-i-cho called Zac-che-us. There was a man in Jer-i-cho called Zac-che-us. Now the He-brews, they were tall, but Zac-che-us, he was small, yet the Lord loved Zac-che-us, bet-ter than them all.

Last time

1. The Lord went walking one day through Jer-i-cho town,

©MCMLXV by Medical Mission Sisters, Philadelphia, Pa.
Sole selling agent Vanguard Music Corp., 250 West 57th St., New York, N.Y. 10019.
All rights reserved. Permission granted to reprint by Vanguard Music Corp.

"Zaccheus" is available on album AVS 101 from Avant Garde Records Inc., 250 W. 57th Street, N.Y., N.Y. 10019

...and the people began to gather from miles around. But Zaccheus, he couldn't see, So he climbed a sycamore tree, And the Lord looked up and said, "Zaccheus, come down." There...

CODA: *...all.*

2. The Lord said: "Zaccheus, I am dining with you today.
   Zaccheus, I come to your house, come lead the way."
   Then Zaccheus, he gave a cheer, but the people began to sneer.
   "This man is a sinner, does the Lord seek lodging here?"

3. Now Zaccheus was small of stature, but he could show,
   that a man who is stout of heart can grow and grow.
   "If I have cheated young and old, I restore the goods fourfold."
   And salvation came that day to his whole household.

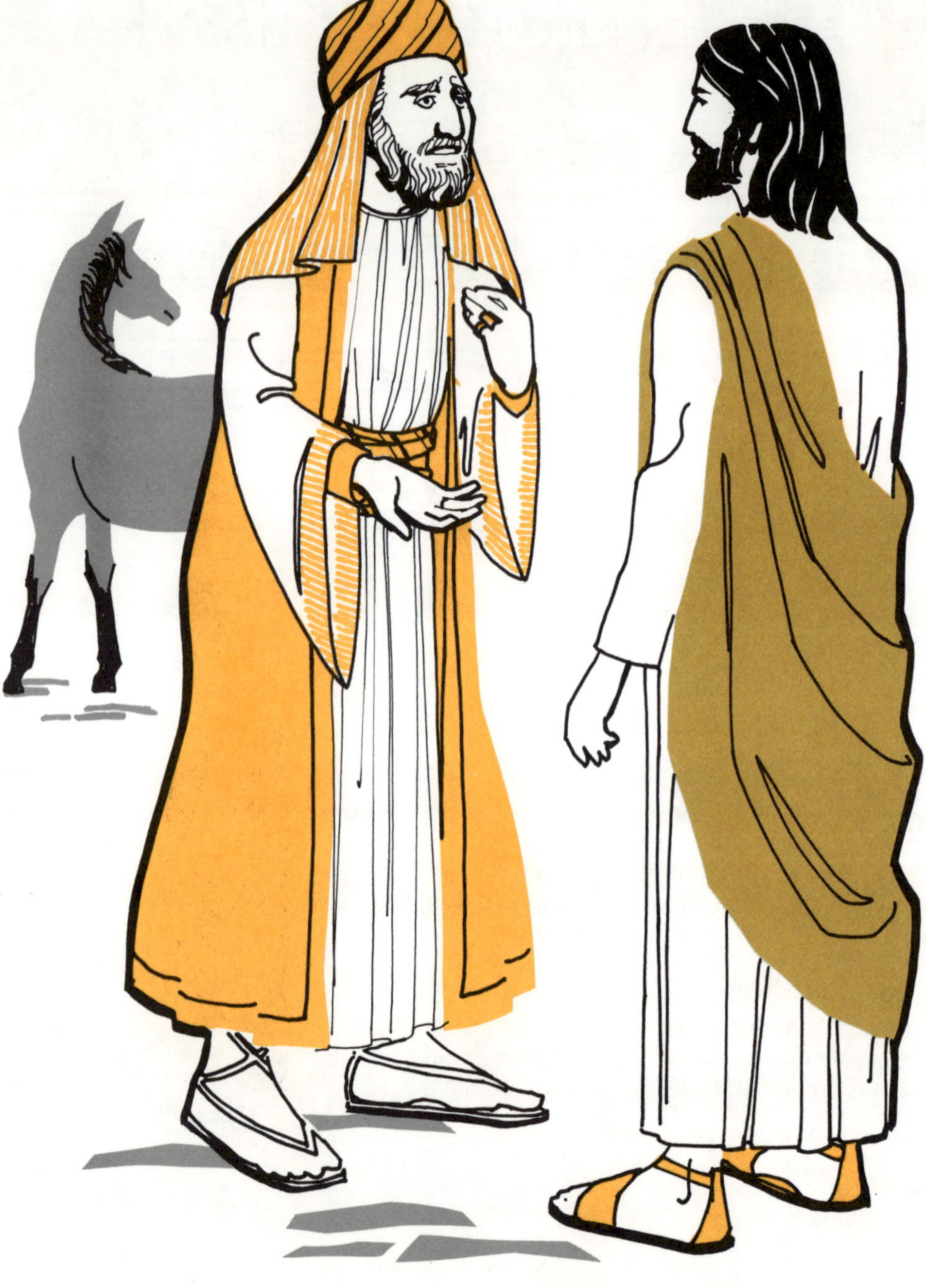

A ONE O'CLOCK MIRACLE

John 4:46-53

NARRATOR: An important officer hurried to see Jesus. He had heard that Jesus was in Cana. It would take him a whole day to get there. He started while it was still dark. As he galloped toward Cana, his horse began to get tired. The officer had to use his horsewhip a few times. After many sweating hours, the aching horse brought its master straight to Jesus. Quickly the officer slid off the side. He stood in front of Jesus, begging excitedly.

OFFICER: Please come with me, Jesus. It's my son. He's sick, I mean really sick! If you come home with me, I know you can heal him.

JESUS: Yes?

OFFICER: But, Jesus, he's about to die. It's an emergency! You must believe me.

JESUS: Do you have to *see* miracles before you will believe in me?

OFFICER: Jesus, please, please come. If we leave right now we can get home before he dies. He's burning with a terrible fever.

JESUS: Go back home, sir. Your son *is* healed.

NARRATOR: For just a minute the officer didn't know what to say. He wasn't expecting this. It was a couple of seconds before he could think straight. Then he spoke.

OFFICER: I believe You, Jesus. If You say that my son is better, then I know that everything is all right. You are the only one who could do this.

NARRATOR: The officer was quietly happy. His body relaxed. A pleasant smile slipped onto his face. He mounted his resting horse. Now there was no need to rush. His precious boy was healed. Jesus said so.

The officer checked the time. It was about one o'clock. He couldn't make it home by dark. So he stayed overnight.

The next morning, he started for home. When he was a short way away, his servants met him.

SERVANTS: Master, master! Your son is better. He's completely well! Is he ever anxious to see you!

OFFICER: Can you tell me what time he started to feel better?

SERVANTS: Yes, we certainly can. It was about

	one o'clock yesterday afternoon.
OFFICER:	One o'clock? That's when I was talking to Jesus. Tell me exactly what happened.
SERVANT:	Well, we'd been watching him closely because he had such a fever.
OFFICER:	Yes, Yes! Go on!
SERVANT:	We checked him again at one. His fever was gone!
OFFICER:	Come with me. We're going home. We've got a lot of talking to do. I know that Jesus is God. I want all of you to know about Him too. It's tremendous. I've never been happier in my life!
NARRATOR:	Not only did the officer believe in God, everyone in his whole house believed in God too!

A RHYTHM STORY — rhythm stories are explained on page 10.

DEATH OF A FRIEND

John 11:1-45

Jesus got a message sage friends:
From two of His best an-y,
"Hur-ry, come to Beth-an-y,
Or Laza-rus's life may end."

But Jesus didn't hur-ry.
In fact, He stayed right there;
Un-til the folks a-round Him said,
"You act like You don't care."

They final-ly went to Beth-an-y
And heard the aw-ful news.
Laz-a-rus was dead four days
And bur-ied in a tomb.

His sis-ters' hearts were bro-ken,
They could-n't help but cry.
The sad-ness of this whole af-fair
Brought tears to Je-sus' eyes.

227

Jesus gave the orders
To roll the stone away.
And while the men were busy
He looked to God and prayed.

While all the people waited,
Jesus gave a shout.
In His loudest voice He called,
"Lazarus, come out!"

Everybody strained to look,
Their mouths were open wide.
It was Lazarus all right —
He walked around inside!

Lazarus came to the door,
Then a-left the grave.
Some believed in God right there
And gave Him all the praise!

JUST IN TIME

Luke 23:39-43

Three men hung on crosses. Hanging on the center cross was Jesus. On each side of Him hung a criminal. People stood below. Some cried quietly Some stared. Others came for the show and chattered among themselves.

The men on the crosses were talking too. One man turned his head toward Jesus. He laughed and teased. "So you're this Messiah, are you? A king, huh? How about proving it a minute? Save yourself! And while you're at it, save us too!"

The other criminal, Dysmas, interrupted him. Don't talk that way. Here you are dying and you dare to speak that way to God? We deserve to die on these crosses. We did some pretty terrible things. But this man . . . He hasn't done anything wrong, not even once!"

Then Dysmas spoke to Jesus. "When you come

to your kingdom, please, Jesus, remember me." He was humble and quiet.

Jesus answered immediately. He knew Dysmas believed He was God.

"Today you and I

will be together

in Paradise.

I promise you this."

Then the three men were quiet. It was noon. Yet it got dark, just as black as night. It was almost spooky. But Dysmas wasn't afraid anymore. He knew he would be with Jesus after he died.

EMPTY CHAINS

Acts 9:1-19

Paul was the strongest Christian-hater you could find. He went to the high priest to get permission to arrest Christians. Wherever Paul went he took chains with him, just in case he found someone who loved Jesus. When he found someone, he was proud and happy about his catch.

One day he left for Damascus. He had the chains with him. He was certain he could find some Christians. He took a couple friends with him to help. But a strange thing happened. Paul never used those chains.

It all took place right outside the city of Damascus. In fact, it happened right in the middle of the road. Paul was hurrying. He was anxious to snoop around town. He had his mind on one thing — arresting Christians!

Suddenly a sparkling, dazzling light hit him like

a spotlight. He fell over backwards from the shock. He covered his eyes, hoping to get out of its powerful path. But he couldn't escape it. Then came the voice.

"Paul, Paul! Why are you trying so hard to hurt me?"

"Who is speaking? Sir, please tell me." Paul rolled over on his stomach, still trying to get away from the light and its glare. His friends looked all around. They saw no one but they could hear the voice.

"I am Jesus," the voice answered loudly. I am the one you are hurting. Now get up and go into the city. Wait there for more directions."

Paul stumbled to his knees. He opened his eyes. But that didn't seem to help. He still couldn't see. He rubbed his eyelids. Still nothing! Paul discovered that he was blind. His eyes were thick and scaly.

Paul's friends had to lead him into town. He stayed at Judas' house, waiting for more directions from God. He waited one day, two days, three whole days! Then God sent word. He sent Ananias to see Paul.

Paul heard the knock on the door. He was hoping for more information. It seemed like such a long time. Paul hadn't had any food or water since it all began. He was eager for company and help.

Ananias walked up to Paul. Ananias laid his hands on Paul's crusty eyes. "Brother Paul, Jesus sent me to you. Yes, He is the same Jesus who met you on the road a few days ago. He sent me over so you may be filled with the Holy Spirit. Your blind eyes will also see again."

Instantly Paul could see! It was as if the crusty, scaly covering fell off his eyes. Immediately he was baptized. He ate supper. He felt great! He could hardly wait to tell the Good News about Jesus!

Perhaps you wonder about the chains. Paul never used them again. He didn't even think about them again. They lay on the side of the road, empty and rusting.

EARTHQUAKE AT MIDNIGHT

Acts 16:25-34

I was getting very tired. It was almost midnight. I had things pretty much under control. I knew I'd better have. If those two men in the inner cell got away, I'd be dead. The judges made that very clear.

Paul and Silas, the two new fellows, were the strangest prisoners I've ever had. They were down there still singing and praying even when it was almost twelve o'clock. I sure couldn't figure out what they had to sing about. They'd been beaten with wooden whips. Their backs were bruised and cut. Blood had dried in the sores. Their feet were in stocks. Yet there they were, singing hymns as if it were a holiday!

I was just about to tell them to quit. They weren't really bothering anyone. In fact, the other prisoners were enjoying it. But I knew that I'd feel better if everyone was asleep or at least if the jail was quiet.

When I had got Paul and Silas quieted down, I lay down. In a few minutes I had dozed off. Suddenly I was jolted awake. I was shaking, I mean really shaking. The doors flew open. I fell over backwards. The bricks came loose. Some pieces were flying around. It sounded like the stocks came loose. I heard chains and handcuffs falling. That was the last I remember. My head hit the floor. It must have knocked me out for just a minute.

When I came to, I was lying on my back. Every single cell door was wide open. Each prisoner had a chance to escape, they were free to run right out of this place. It seemed as if I was the only one around. Then I remembered my orders. If Paul and Silas ever got away, I would die!

I raised my sword. I would rather have killed myself than let the judges do it. In the quiet and darkness of the prison, I was ready to die.

A voice interrupted me. I jerked. "Don't do that! Please don't! All of us are here!"

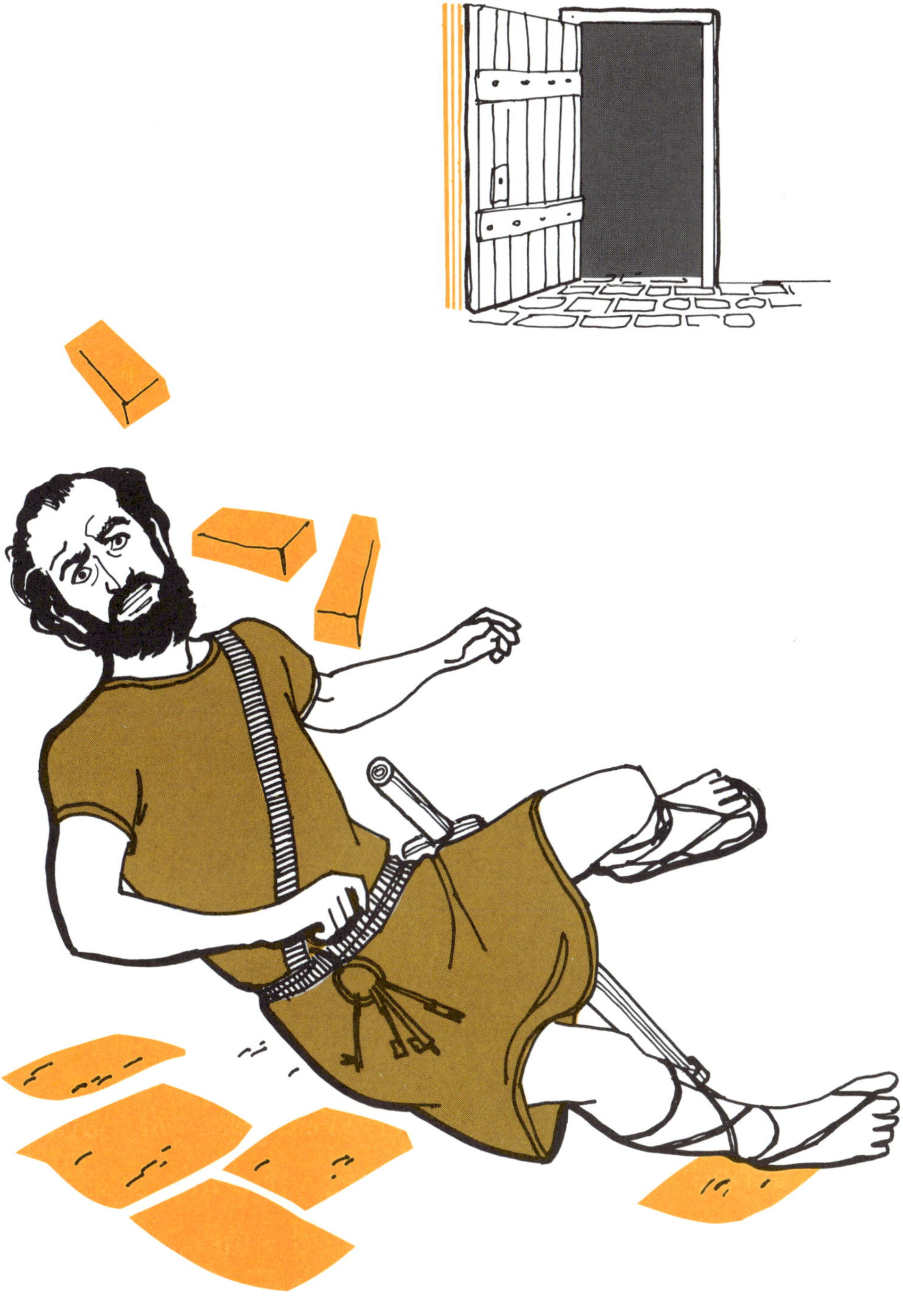

What a nightmare! That whole night had been strange. First the prisoners were singing. Then the earthquake came. Now this voice called from the prison cell. I was still shaking when I ordered that the lamp be lit again. I ran toward the voice. It had come from Paul's and Silas's cell. I was positive that only their God could do such a thing as this!

"Sirs," I begged them. "What do I have to do to be saved?"

"Believe on Jesus and you will be saved."

There sat Paul and Silas . . . the stocks had fallen over. Their handcuffs were on the floor. Their backs were aching and sore.

"I believe! I do! I do!" I cried it right out, over and over again. I was still shaking. Only now it was from joy, pure joy!

I ran to call my family. We were all baptized. I washed the cuts and sores of Paul and Silas. I used warm water. That would make the torn skin and aching muscles feel better. How I wanted to help them. Then I brought them home. My wife fixed a big dinner, chicken and biscuits. Poor Paul and Silas hadn't eaten like that in days. So we just kept passing the food to them.

The next day the judges sent a message for me to let Paul and Silas go. How thankful I was to meet them and to learn to know their God . . . my God!

Opinions and doctrines expressed in this book/video are those of the author and do not necessarily reflect those of the Wisconsin Evangelical Lutheran Synod, Holy Trinity Evangelical Lutheran Church, or its pastor or faculty.